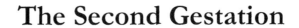

The Second Gestation

The Second Gestation

The Life and Death of a Doctor's Daughter

Amanda Wharton

For
Rose

All those involved in Rose's journey are thanked in the text. The wonderful support I got from friends and family kept me going. I would like to make a special mention of the District Nurses, the unsung heroes of Palliative Care.

My friend Netia Mayman was the first person to read and comment on the script. Thank you Netia for your careful reading and for your belief in me and in the project without which I probably wouldn't have continued.

Nicola Wyld also read and commented at a later stage, thank you for your helpful comments.

Jan Date suggested the title, thank you.

Finally, thanks to my son, David Rowthorn, who helped me with the IT issues and designed the cover for me.

INTRODUCTION 1

CHAPTER 1   Rose 4

CHAPTER 2   Illness 11

CHAPTER 3   Paliative Care... 23

CHAPTER 4   A Brief Look at Asbestos........................... 28

CHAPTER 5   What is Peritoneal Mesothelioma?......... 37

CHAPTER 6   Do Not Resuscitate................................... 46

CHAPTER 7   More Positive Times 50

CHAPTER 8   What is Empathy...................................... 55

CHAPTER 9   Friends and Family 61

CHAPTER 10   The End of the Reprieve 65

CHAPTER 11   Assisted Dying 69

CHAPTER 12   The Last Days... 75

CHAPTER 13   Our Journey Together 78

CHAPTER 14   After Life Has Ended 81

CHAPTER 15   The Future of Medicine........................... 86

EPILOGUE 89

INTRODUCTION

We listen to stories in the news, from friends and acquaintances about people whose lives change forever within a single moment in time. We contemplate it for a few seconds, note how devastating it must be, and then we move on; it's forgotten. My life changed forever on a sunny day in August 2017. It will never be forgotten. I will strive continuously to move on.

This is the story of the diagnosis of my daughter's terminal illness, living through the illness with her, her death and the aftermath. As a doctor, carer and mother, this was a complicated journey.

My experiences as a General Practitioner and the patient stories that I would like to tell are now all jumbled in my memory. General Practice is a rich source of the history, sociology and psychology of a society and its members. I have often regretted that I did not record these peoples' stories as I encountered them and they are lost. Many different parts of these stories have, however, been internalised.

The story of the illness and death of my daughter, Rose, at the age of thirty-three is a rich one. The personal journey of Rose, and all who were touched by her, is one that I felt should be written so as not to be lost as so many other stories have been. Writing the book of her journey was also, of course, a catharsis for me who, as mother, carer and doctor, had to record the journey. It is not only for me. I have tried to make this a story of interest to the general reader and one from which all doctors and medical professionals and students can learn.

I am not the first to write such a book. I was inspired to do so after reading three books that came out of the USA: the first, *Being Mortal* by Atul Gawande[1], I had read a few years ago. The other two I encountered, by chance and from *The Times*' reviews. They are *When*

---

[1] Atul Gawande. Being Mortal: Illness, Medicine and What Matters in the End. Profile Books 2014

Breath becomes Air by Paul Kalanithi[2] and *In Shock* by Rana Awdish[3]. The first is by a neurosurgeon who was diagnosed with terminal cancer at the age of thirty-six and the second details the experiences of a doctor who spent many weeks in Intensive Care and could hear the professionals' conversations about her. All these doctors were forced to confront the ways they themselves communicated with patients and all became wiser. I would recommend any doctor, student doctor or interested lay person to read these inspiring but very different books.

In a similar way, through my experience with Rose, I was led to think about the ways I have spoken to patients, my assumptions about them, my prejudices, how they may have received my consultation and also my successes. As a GP trained in the UK and as a trainer of GPs, communication skills have always been a fulcrum around which consultations take place. I considered myself a 'good communicator' but have reassessed this in the light of sharing my daughter's experiences of the medical profession: questioning the way people spoke to her made me realise that I myself had probably displayed some of the same inadequacies at some time in my career.

I'm sure Rose would have hated the idea of me writing this book. In a way, she hated making a fuss and was quick to be kind to others but not always to herself. I will feel justified if it succeeds in prompting readers to consider the way they communicate with those who have illnesses or face death. This includes anyone with a relative, friend or colleague in that challenging situation. It also, vitally, includes doctors and other medical practitioners who have a responsibility of care in the way that they communicate with their patients. The effect our words have on others can be devastating. Much of what I observed as I accompanied Rose on this journey disappointed me. I may sound critical of my colleagues, and as a fellow doctor I understand the pressures clinicians are under. Throughout, though, there were shining examples of thoughtful consulting, fantastic communication skills, empathy and kindness.

---

[2] Paul Kalanithi. When Breath becomes Air. Vintage 2016
[3] Rana Awdish. In Shock: How nearly dying made me a better doctor. Transworld 2019

I was a parent before I knew anything about medicine. This is not due to being a teenage parent but because I had a former life as a teacher and then researcher. I came to medicine late in life, qualifying as an MB BChir at age forty-two. When I started the long journey into medicine, my children were five and three.

Having had more life experiences than the average medical student, I had advantages over them, not least in how seriously I took my studies. I like to think I became a better doctor more quickly than my peers. Having children certainly makes one grow up.

After qualifying, working long shifts, sometimes in distant towns, was a challenge to our family life. But my husband, Bob, took on his role as main carer alongside his academic job without much complaint. I think the stresses of this life weighed heavily on us as a couple, and the children almost certainly suffered from not having their mum around much. Despite these pressures, the family did survive and the children grew up to be secure and wonderful adults.

I have loved my job as a GP and have always been in awe of what people will tell me, how they trust me and how grateful they can be about small things I can do for them. My life as a GP certainly affected how I responded to the many clinicians we encountered, as well as to Rose, throughout her illness.

In this book I tell Rose's story and start by giving readers an insight into what kind of person she was so as to give the story more meaning. I also talk about our journey together through the illness. On this meandering path, I am attempting to illustrate the importance of communication, not only within the clinical consultation but as something we can all learn from and use in our day-to-day lives. I am perhaps over-critical of my colleagues, but I do recognise that not all patients are easy to communicate with effectively. It is certainly a skill I continue to learn.

Throughout, the story is interrupted by looking at other issues which are relevant. Thus, I look at the debate on assisted dying; I have a discussion of the philosophical basis of empathy. I look at the asbestos industry worldwide and I have a more medical chapter on the disease that killed her – mesothelioma. These chapters can be read in the order I put them, or they can be left to the end for those who do not wish to break the narrative.

3

CHAPTER 1
Rose

When people die, everyone seems to come out of the woodwork to say how wonderful they were: I have always found it hard to believe that each of these people, described in such glowing terms, could really be so amazing! If I am to tell you about my daughter, my relationship with her and the family dynamics as a whole, it must be in a frank and honest way, including the good parts and the challenges. I am aware that this is my opinion, that Rose cannot offer us her own view of herself and her relationships with us. I don't have many insights into her view as it was not something we ever really talked about. I wish we had.

I often struggled with Rose's behaviour as a child and early teenager, as no doubt she struggled with her relationship with me and the family. From my viewpoint, Rose had a complicated personality: as a child and teenager she was stubborn and feisty. Some may describe her as a 'drama queen'. At the same time, she was very brave in physical challenges and had a noticeable level of perseverance. She was also loving and thoughtful and would have given her life to protect her baby brother, except when she wanted to kill him! As a child and young teen, she had a difficult relationship with her father, Bob, and her brother, David. I think there was a lot of jealousy there, and a lack of confidence. She always had to have the last word, and I often remonstrated with Bob that he was supposed to be the adult, not another child! David was often upset by the conflicts they had, as was Rose, but they seemed unable to extricate themselves from battles. As David grew up, he learnt to remove himself from conflictual situations, physically and mentally. Despite these difficulties in the family dynamics, Rose bore no grudges and loved her father and brother dearly. My own relationship with her could also be stormy, not least because I often felt like a referee in the family battles. But I do not think that we were necessarily atypical as a family, and children with strong characters must always fight their corner.

For many reasons, I don't think Rose was a very happy child. When I first wrote this I had no evidence for it, just a mother's instinct.

Sometime after her death I happened upon a letter she had, obviously, never sent to a friend whereby she expressed her unhappiness, confirming my instincts.

Rose was a keenly awaited baby. I had two miscarriages before her and then it took a while to get pregnant again. , After the first difficult twelve weeks of 'colic', she was a good sleeper as a baby. She was quite sedentary, not learning to crawl and only moving when she started to walk at thirteen months. This gave her time to perfect her spatial skills and she loved to do puzzles and fitting shapes in boxes. In fact, I made her a 'puzzle cake' for her second birthday and have a lovely photo of her, knife in hand, ready to cut it – although it was already cut! She was very pleased with the effort!

Rose also displayed her stubbornness at an early age and was not easily distracted from what she wanted! When David arrived eighteen months after her, she was very happy to have a plaything. As he got older and presented more of a threat to her cosy world, she found it difficult to adapt. There is much written about how a child's position in a family may affect their personality and that of their siblings. I am not familiar with this body of work, but in my own family and those of several friends, I have noticed that it is the oldest child who often has the most difficulties. Whether this might be due to sibling rivalry or to the inexperience of new parents or much more complicated interactions I do not know.

Back to Rose. She went to full-time nursery from the age of six months. When she was one, we went to live in Canberra for three months as Bob had got a research sabbatical there. Afterwards, we travelled to Queensland, where Rose celebrated her first birthday. I knew by this time that I was pregnant again.

Back in Cambridge, David joined her in the nursery when he was six months old and I went back to my teaching job in a local secondary school.

Three years later we went to live in Sydney for six months as Bob had another teaching fellowship. Rose and David both loved the outside life and the freedom the good weather gave them. Rose, in particular, loved swimming. We had good friends there and it was a wonderful time. The children went part time to a nursery, as Rose was not old enough for school in Australia, and I continued with the research I had been doing, turning my PhD into a book (sadly never published!). Some may think that all this travel was disruptive to the family life, but I think it instilled in Rose a love of travel and curiosity about people in other societies.

When we returned to Cambridge in the Summer of 1988, Rose started school. She was the youngest in her class (having been born on 30th August), but she was probably the tallest. There has been a lot of research about how children develop at school and their success in relation to their birthdate. It is generally agreed that summer-born babies have more difficulty due to their early start. [4] I think everybody treated Rose as older than she was, and therefore expected more from her, because of her birthdate and the fact she was so tall.

I was at a loss about what to do myself, not wanting to go back to teaching. The idea to do medicine came out of a discussion with Bob who thought I would be well suited to being a doctor. In fact, he said, "Why don't you do what you've always wanted to and become a doctor?" This took me aback, because I had never realised that I had wanted to follow this career. I had always assumed it was closed to me due to my schooling and not very memorable results. It certainly struck a chord when he said this.

I had to do A levels again to get the right subjects and then nearly six years of medical school. It was hard for me, but I think it was hard on the children too. Bob was great as he had to be the main carer, mixing this with his academic job. We had au pairs – some fantastic, some not really able to cope with these very headstrong children. I do think the children suffered from not having their mother around much, and I keenly remember one morning David sitting on the stairs and sobbing, begging me not to go to work. Rose just used to say I was never there when she got home from school and never made cakes for tea like proper mums!

Whilst trying to write a eulogy to Rose, which my brother, Tony, read at her funeral, some memories I reflected on were amusing, in retrospect, and illustrated her determined personality. An anecdote in this eulogy indeed raised a subdued laugh. When she was four or five, I remember going to buy some new shoes for her in the local shop; my

---

[4] https://schoolsweek.co.uk/summer-borns-still-struggle-in-year-6-and-3-other-findings-from-primary-schools-test-results-analysis/

mother came too. Rose chose some shoes but they didn't have them in her size so she refused to put on her old shoes and crawled out of the shop and along the street, crying out that her mum wouldn't buy her any shoes! My poor mother was mortified. Another recollection happened at the doctor's surgery. I used to collect them from the after-school playcentre on my bicycle with a front and back seat (none of these great bike-carriages we see now on the road!). She had refused to put her shoes on (again!) and, as we travelled, she put her bare foot in the front spokes of the bicycle. She had lifted her foot off the metal bar that was digging into it. Everyone went flying off the bike. Fortunately, David was fine but Rose had a nasty wound on her foot. Interestingly, not a single car stopped to see if we were OK – we were on the pavement of a bridge over the river Cam. I was mortified that I had not been more successful at persuading her to put her shoes on. Rose just escaped having to have plastic surgery on her foot and had to use crutches so that it could heal. When we suggested, a few weeks later, that she didn't actually need the crutches anymore, she was not keen to give them up. At the doctor's surgery she was making the most of her proficiency with the crutches, playing to the waiting patients. Her 'favourite' GP (the only one she would see) looked at her foot and said, "Well, Rose, I'm pleased to say you don't need your crutches anymore." She jumped up and ran down the stairs, Bob following, telling everyone in the waiting room they had just witnessed a 'miracle cure', much to everyone's amusement.

These amusing anecdotes give a clue to a personality that was very determined. She was also very brave, always giving things a go and persevering when many others would have given up. She was physically courageous, even if I could tell she was scared. These attributes stood her in good stead for what she had to endure in her illness. She persevered with horse riding and it became part of our annual holiday in Wales. The last time we all went, there was a hilarious scene where we were trotting on the common and both Rose's and David's horses stopped dead in their tracks at the same time, sending both children flying over the horses' heads. They got back on again, to their credit. Unfortunately, as he was later cantering around the yard, Bob was thrown, knocked out cold and broke his thumb. He had concussion and ended up in hospital and I think that scared the children more than their own falls. This self-challenging streak continued throughout her life, with rock climbing, football, skiing and hang gliding as examples. She was always game to give it a go even though she wasn't naturally very good at these things, especially when compared to her brother. Swimming was really the only thing she was very good at and which felt natural to her – she was a water baby. Whenever we went away together, it always had to be somewhere where we could swim. When Rose was about twelve, we got a Labrador puppy to cure her from her extraordinary fear of dogs, which on one occasion almost led her to jump into the sea off a pier to get away from a dog. Once our puppy, Laurel, was grown up, she came with us on our annual holiday to the Gower Peninsular. Rose used to love swimming with Laurel who would follow her and race her through the waves, always 'protecting' Rose.

As a teenager, Rose had many friends at school, but her group were not the 'cool' gang. They didn't wear trendy clothes or go out at night all made up and looking twice their age. Probably due to this there was a certain amount of bullying. Rose always stood up for herself and did get into many arguments with friends and others. I remember she even missed one of her GCSE exams because she had a physical fight on the way to school; she came home upset and refused to go back to school to take the exam. Feisty she definitely was, but as I said, I do not think she was a very happy older child and teenager. She often stood on the outside of groups when she didn't have her friends with her, like on holiday, but once she was accepted into the group, she was much happier. I think that this experience of being an 'outsider' helped make her such an amazingly generous adult when she identified other people in the same predicament. She was always careful to invite people to join in, especially in her work as a youth leader in the church, particularly with overseas students. Many people who made comments in the book I put out at her funeral mentioned how Rose had helped them when they were new to the town or church or were unhappy.

Rose felt she was always under the shadow of her brother. He found life easier and was naturally very talented at sports and academically, although in terms of the latter he never put enough effort in. They had some hefty fights. All through her childhood, though, I believe she felt loved and valued by her parents and could be delightful company. She started to go to church with Bob when she was about thirteen. Bob was not a 'believer', but he had always thought that

8

belonging to a group was important, having himself been a Queen's Scout and a member of various political parties. Rose enjoyed this time with her father, and when she was a bit older, she started going to a different church on her own, becoming baptised when she was seventeen. Church and her Christian faith became a major part of her life. She found solace in Jesus, I am sure, and although a lapsed Catholic myself, and therefore rather cynical, I thank God for this.

Rose studied maths and chemistry for her A levels and won a place at Newcastle University. She had a gap year first and went off to Argentina with a Christian organisation. She helped build a school in Salta and then worked in an orphanage. She loved children and they loved her. This theme continued throughout her young adulthood when friend after friend got pregnant: she was always Auntie Rose. I think it was a sadness to her that she had no partner and thus no children. She was so looking forward to being a proper auntie to David and Harriet's children.

After graduating, she worked in the EU farming subsidy office in Newcastle for a while, then came home and worked on the wards in Addenbrookes Hospital and then as a researcher for a professor at the hospital. She decided to go on to do Medical Statistics at Leicester University. In truth, I think she wanted to be a doctor, despite seeing how hard it had been for me and how this had impacted on her own life but she never had enough faith in herself that she would get into medical school. She was a real 'people person'. She would have made a great doctor.

She graduated from Leicester with a merit in her MSc. She then got a university job in Oxford as a medical statistician and, after a couple of years, got a more senior post in the Nuffield Department of Clinical Neurosciences where she became a sought-after statistician by doctors who needed help with their statistics for their PhDs. She worked on many papers which were published in prestigious journals but she remained humble about her work. She became a very well-liked team member and was known for her lively repartee and sense of humour. It is a fantastic tribute to her that her colleagues assembled all the papers she had been involved in and produced a beautiful bound 'book' for us. I was really touched by this and it made me realise just how loved she was. Her church, St Ebbe's in Headington, was very important to her, though she did not accept all the evangelical doctrine uncritically. She often complained to me that the church had a very traditional view of women's roles in the church and in the family: my feminism had obviously rubbed off on her! Her many friends delighted in her company and she was often the life and soul of the party in her many holidays and outings with them. I think that she was really very happy with her life in Oxford and had developed into a secure, loveable, amazingly clever and rounded person.

Although Rose had many close friends, she did not have a partner. I never understood this as she was attractive, lively, funny and intelligent. She had many male friends and she was not gay (she told me about being approached by a couple of members of her football team!). Although she was quite a feminist in her own way, as I said above, she was a bit of a traditionalist also and felt unable to initiate any potential relationship. So, when she became ill, there was no partner to look after her. Her family, especially myself, had no choice but to step into that role. I have no regrets about the loss of my own independent life in Cambridge. It is what mothers do, and at least I could be the mother she perhaps had missed when she was growing up. But don't get me wrong, it wasn't done out of a sense of guilt or duty. It was such a precious time for me, and hopefully for her. At first, of course, I did not know exactly how things would unfold but I don't think I ever gave a second thought to having to leave work and friends. Later, I will tell the story of our journey together through this terrible time.

CHAPTER 2

Illness

The story of Rose's illness and how it changed all our lives begins in the summer of 2017. Rose and I went to our flat in Italy, on Lake Como. We had a tradition of going on a 'mother and daughter' holiday every year. We usually went abroad as we both liked the sun and swimming and were content to read away the days, swim and eat nice meals. There were the inevitable niggly arguments, but we loved going away together and always came back for more.

The flat on the lake was great for swimming, but as she said, "You can't go anywhere without walking uphill." This time she made a bit more of this and I got a bit irritated with her for being feeble, not really registering that she was, in fact, getting very short of breath going uphill. Rose was always an active and fit person and she was rarely ill. I am ashamed that I did not recognise that she was struggling and that she didn't feel able to tell me. If she had been a friend, I would have been concerned and sympathetic. Instead, I was quietly frustrated, thinking she was making a fuss.

About four weeks after this holiday Rose came home for a birthday visit. She was 33. She said her colleagues and friends had commented that she had lost weight. They had also noticed that she seemed tired and sometimes fell asleep at her desk. We went to the sports' centre together – her to swim and I went to the gym. I was shocked at how thin she looked and she told me afterwards that she had only been able swim ten lengths and had to keep stopping, whereas normally she would swim forty lengths straight off. All the alarm bells went off in my head and I persuaded her that she must make an appointment with her GP. She then told me that she had also been sweating quite a lot at night. She agreed to go to the GP when she got back to Oxford, but of course, in her usual way of not wanting to make a fuss (or perhaps out of fear?), made a 'routine' appointment a week ahead.

Later, Rose openly wondered whether her life could have been saved if she had gone to the GP earlier. We discussed this and I told her that an earlier presentation of rather insubstantial symptoms would probably not have prompted an urgent response. Also, this awful disease presents very late and even if it had been discovered two or three months earlier, it would not have been treatable. She would probably just have had the knowledge that she was going to die for longer: not something most people would want.

I have always found it a curiosity how different people react to illness. Many, especially in my experience, older patients tend to wait as they don't want to 'bother the doctor'. I have had at least one patient who died as a result of waiting a weekend with chest pain and another who waited with melena (bleeding from the bowel) and was so shut down that the paramedic and I struggled to find a vein to start fluids that would keep her alive until she got to hospital. Yet others make it a weekly event to go to the GP and tell the same, or rotating, symptoms they cannot accept reassurance about. Rose had a few friends who had conditions that seemed to dominate their lives and their personalities and she did not want to be like that. But, of course, it is also fear that keeps some people away from the medics, and indeed makes some attend every week. I have always found the psychology of illness behaviour fascinating, but sometimes, when faced with the same person, week after week, complaining of symptoms that have been fully investigated, it is a test of my patience. But these patients with medically unexplained symptoms are becoming a category in themselves (DSM 5) and there is now a burgeoning literature about this.[5]

Of course, we sometimes get it wrong, and no medical person can argue that we understand everything about illness (though some may think that they themselves do!). Most people, even those with health anxiety, will respond to being listened to and to kindness.

But, unfortunately, Rose had symptoms that were alarming to me as a doctor, with several 'red flags' (what we call symptoms that might indicate a serious problem).

---

[5] E.g. How should we manage adults with persistent unexplained physical symptoms?
BMJ 2017; 356

At a late Monday afternoon appointment after work, she saw a GP trainee who, after listening to the story and examining her, called in her supervisor. I am grateful that this trainee did not just tell Rose she had a chest infection and send her home with antibiotics. She had a significant fever, over 38 degrees, and quiet breath sounds. As a GP trainer myself, I know that many trainees are extremely competent and careful, taking less risks than those more experienced doctors who recognise patterns and pick up red flags quickly. But there are also those who believe they can go it alone and make mistakes which have to be rectified later, after discussion with their trainer. This GP registrar sent her up to the Emergency Evaluation Unit for blood tests. When the test results came in, the doctor went to see her and told her that they were 'very abnormal' and that she would have to stay in overnight at least. We were later told that her CRP was over 600, her haemoglobin was 73, her albumin was 18 and her platelets were very high. These numbers will only be understandable to my medical readers, but they basically meant that she had extremely high markers for infection or inflammation, was very anaemic, and severely malnourished. Nobody could understand how she was functioning at all, let alone going to work. She was admitted to the John Radcliffe Hospital.

Subsequent X-rays and a CT scan showed pleural and cardiac effusions (collection of fluid around the lungs and the heart) and a thickening of the small bowel.

My own 'differential diagnosis' had initially been TB (tuberculosis, formerly known as consumption, and now rare in this country but more widespread in Asia) as she had been to Sri Lanka, living with a local family 18 months before, or lymphoma/leukaemia (a type of blood cancer). This is the point at which my roles first became entwined. I was, of course, primarily a mother. But I could not stop being a doctor. As such, over the course of the next nine months, doors opened that may not have done otherwise, disasters were prevented. Perhaps this is also why I could distance myself emotionally in order to be able to cope with Rose's inevitable decline. I dealt with emergency situations that needed a cool head and a level of organisation I may not have had without my medical training. As doctors we are taught to respond immediately to emergencies, to be always thinking about diagnosis and disease presentation. We often forget we are dealing with a human being with fears and expectations. Now I was forced into doing my best to fulfil two roles. The dual role of doctor and mother took its toll. It complicated our relationship and I'm not sure it was emotionally good for either of us. Most of the time I was able to be just her mum, and hopefully Rose felt loved in that way. I could not help also being the doctor, and just as I don't know how it would have been if I had not been a doctor in that situation, it will be hard for the reader to understand how it was to have that dual role. So many people have to go through the experience of watching a loved one die that any attempt to understand that situation must be worthwhile. Hopefully, I can help with this through my story.

Bob and I went down to Oxford as soon as we heard she was in hospital. She seemed outwardly cheerful, sitting up in bed, entertaining the droves of colleagues and friends who came to see her. Over the next week or so, she saw doctors from practically every specialty there was – except geriatrics and obstetrics! She saw gastroenterologists, general surgeons, respiratory physicians, infectious disease doctors, general medics and when an operation was deemed necessary, a cardiologist. Every time she saw a new doctor – and there is now very little consistency in ward doctors due to the changes that the European Union working directive on the number of hours a person can work prescribed – she had to tell her story again. I have been a patient myself and got very frustrated by this retelling of the story to different grades of doctor and different specialities, but this was nothing compared to what Rose had to go through and I could see how much it frustrated and tired her. However, she remained polite and answered everything with great patience. I found it hard to play my part as doctor/mother. I tried not to talk too much and not to become the person the doctor spoke to instead of speaking to Rose, but I also wanted to ask questions that I didn't think Rose would know to ask, despite being an intelligent person working on the periphery of medicine in the John Radcliffe. I always left when she was being examined. I tried to look for clues in her face as to how I should behave, but often got it wrong and ended up getting her sharp tongue. I knew that behind the bravado she was very frightened. I felt frustrated when doctors or nurses couldn't find a vein to take blood or put in a cannula, resisting the temptation to say anything or to suggest I do it myself! But I understand that those clinicians who knew I was a doctor probably felt a bit nervous with me there so I ended up just leaving the bedside. Anyway, there was no way Rose would have let me – quite rightly! One of her rules that became more important as things progressed was that she would not allow me to do anything that would cause her pain. It was very important to her, and became increasingly so, that I was first and foremost her mum and mothers did not hurt their children.

It was interesting for me to see how different doctors spoke to Rose. Some were lovely, others were detached, some were ignorant of her case and had not read the notes before coming to see her. One Saturday, a consultant she had not met before, who was obviously 'on duty', clearly had no idea about her case and said vastly inappropriate things: the junior doctor who was with him even made a point of coming to see her after the ward round to give her the time she needed to discuss things and to apologise. Many of the doctors coming around offered some suggestions about diagnosis: I remember one in particular saying, "We hope it's TB." Rose picked this up, adding in for herself the unsaid continuation of the sentence ... "because that is treatable."

Bob and I went back to Cambridge as we had various commitments. Rose's friends continued to be with her a lot of the time, which I think she secretly found quite tiring, but would not say so. The medical teams were baffled and so it was decided that she should have a laparoscopy to look inside her abdomen and pelvis and take biopsies of the thickened lining they had seen on the CT scan. They were a bit anxious about her pericardial effusion (the fluid around the heart) and she was scared witless by a visit from the Intensive Care doctor who thought she would need to go to the Intensive Care Unit post-operatively – an example of the effect of words spoken without a thought as to their effect, and there were many more examples of this to come. As it turned out, a cardiologist did an echocardiogram (a scan of the heart) and decided the effusion was small and not likely to be a factor. She had the surgery and there were no complications.

About two days later, when she had been in hospital ten days, I got a phone call from her phone. It was a good friend of hers, Anna, who was a nurse and was sitting with her because she was visiting her in her break. Anna said that Rose was very upset and had asked her to call me to tell me to come back to Oxford: she had cancer.

15

So how did Rose learn of her diagnosis? A consultant surgeon, whom she had never met before, came on his ward round and asked her the same old questions. Then about five minutes later he came back, stood at the end of the bed and said, "We have your biopsy results – you have cancer." He then went on to tell her it was 'peritoneal mesothelioma' and left. Poor Rose was distressed and called one of her colleagues who was working in the same unit as Rose in another wing of the hospital. Of course, Aubretia went to her straight away. Anna arrived a few minutes later. When Anna phoned, she told me what had happened, including the matter-of-fact but terrifying diagnosis Rose had been given. The word 'mesothelioma' went through me like a knife because I knew, instantly, that this was a severe disease with little hope of survival. I don't know to this day how I managed that drive to Oxford, how I could concentrate on the notorious M25, negotiating traffic jams and crazily fast drivers; it was as if there was an external hand safely steering my car.

When Bob and I got to the ward, Rose seemed calm and Anna was still with her. I felt like I was in a vice, shoulders aching, trying to keep back the tears. Although I knew about the disease, mesothelioma, I had never heard of it being in the peritoneum, the lining of the abdomen encasing all the organs. At this point I did not know the ways this disease would develop or what symptoms Rose would have to suffer. Rose immediately told me I must not Google it and to tell David not to either. Needless to say, I did look into it as it was not something I had ever come across. David scanned all the medical journals he could access, and despite not being medical, his academic brain helped him to understand all the consequences of this disease. Rose was scared. She was no longer crying, but her face was immobile; no smile, no more jokes. She told me that she had known for a few days that it was not going to be good news, not going to be TB, for example. She said, "I knew they (the doctors) were all thinking it was something like cancer because no one made any positive comments. If you have something curable then doctors are always positive." This is a good insight into the dilemma doctors face when they believe the news will be bad. It is something I am very aware of, having been in the situation of uncertainty myself. For example, in the seemingly simple task of sending a woman with a breast lump to have it looked at. I know if it is most likely to be cancer due to the nature of the lump and I know if it's most likely benign, although there are many in between we cannot, as GPs with no other tests like a mammogram, be sure of. If we think it is benign, we say we are being cautious. What do we say if we think it is cancer? Many training sessions are spent practising breaking bad news, and the line between offering hope and giving false reassurance is a fine one to tread. This is a dilemma that is discussed by Kathryn Mannix in her insightful and often heart-rending book *With the End in Mind: Dying, Death, and Wisdom in an Age of Denial.*[6] Like Rose, I think many patients pick up what we think. One thing is for sure though, if I have a serious diagnosis to tell someone I do not do so in the way Rose was told the news by the surgeon. Rose was as upset as me about the scenario, though she hid it by telling it as an 'amusing' story to her friends.

It is difficult to fathom why some doctors are good at breaking news and others seem not to be. There is the issue of the doctor protecting themselves – bad news can be incredibly sad and when we give it to patients, especially those we know well, it can be very upsetting to us as doctors. A more distant approach is a way of protecting ourselves, and also, perhaps, our patients who do not want to break down in front of us. But I'm afraid there are too many doctors who just don't know how to do it. Henry Marsh, in his book *Do No Harm*, describes how he approached a patient well known to him: "I walked around the bed and, with my knees cracking, knelt down beside him. To stand over your dying patient would be as inhumane as the long hospital corridors." Also, "I have learnt over the years that when breaking bad news, as it is called, it is probably best to speak as little as possible … I must overcome my urge to talk and talk to fill the sad silence."[7] I will come back to this theme when discussing the concept of empathy. In fact, it is a theme which runs through most of this book because I have thought about this throughout my career, not least when I am acting as a trainer of young GPs. I don't claim to get it right every time.

---

[6] Kathryn Mannix. With the End in Mind: Dying , Death and Wisdom in an Age of Denial. Harper Collins 2017

[7] Henry Marsh. Do No Harm: Stories of Life, Death and Brain Surgery. St Martin's Press 2015

So now Rose had a diagnosis; I think it was 4th of September. She was seen by yet more doctors, the oncologists (cancer doctors) and the palliative care team (end of life care doctors). Before she left the hospital, she was given a blood transfusion. She was so happy to be home in her Oxford flat after two weeks in hospital.

I had thrown a suitcase together when I left for Oxford that terrible day of hearing the news and I did not go back to Cambridge until Christmas when Rose asked if she could go 'home' for Christmas, always a very important family event for her. I moved into her spare bedroom and I was luckily able to rent a flat in the same complex: a stroke of luck that Rose, with her strong faith, did not believe was a coincidence. The other flat meant that Bob could stay down, and also David and his wife, Harriet, and anyone else who wanted to come and needed a bed.

She had an appointment with the oncologist fairly soon after leaving hospital. That interval was one where she still had hope and was up for the fight. She even talked to me about harvesting her eggs before she had any chemotherapy so she always had the option to have a child. The selfish part of me wishes that Rose had had a child before she died, that she had known the amazing love that a mother feels for their child. It would have been so good if a part of Rose, her child, had lived on to give me some solace. But, of course, that would have meant more grief for her, mythical, husband and child. Paul Kalanithi, in *When Breath becomes Air*, talks about this, and he did manage to have a daughter, post diagnosis, who he shared a few precious months with.

Looking back, this was a precious time as she was still my daughter, still the same old Rose. Sitting in the clinic waiting room, she commented on how old everyone there was. This was something she always found difficult; the fact that she was so young and still had her life before her made it harder to bear. In that waiting room, before her first post-diagnosis appointment, I gave her my mother's antique ruby ring which my grandmother had given to my mother and I had been given when I was forty. Rose really liked it and I had promised her that she would have it when she was forty. I knew that she never would be forty, and so I gave it to her to wear. She thanked me but made no other comment. It was somehow reassuring to see that family heirloom on her finger and she never took it off. It is now back on my finger.

In the consultation with the oncologist and the specialist nurse, I sat next to Rose. I was conscious that she was very nervous, anxious and upset, but was keeping her self-control. It would have been so easy to allow the doctor to talk to me instead of to Rose, as she was not really engaging in the conversation. As a GP I have always been conscious of the need to speak to the patients as much as possible, even if they are a child or an elderly person with some cognitive decline. This is drummed into us as GPs but I have witnessed that many fail to do it. I tried to avoid eye contact with the consultant, despite her attempts to make contact with me. Rose sat there stony-faced. The consultant talked about having chemotherapy and explained it to Rose, although through her work on clinical trials Rose knew quite a bit about it already. The consultant said, "If you have chemotherapy, we are looking at three to twelve months." She continued to expand that chemo may shrink the tumour but that it was not a cure: in fact, there was no cure. I watched Rose's face turn pale and rigid. I instinctively put my hand on her arm but she shrugged me off. I only spoke to the consultant when Rose asked me to. There were no tears from her and I controlled mine except when she was behind the curtain being examined. A couple of months later when Rose was going through her 'angry' phase[8], she said to me, "Why did the doctor tell me the prognosis? I didn't ask her to, she just told me." Thus, for the second time, bad news was broken to her in a way which was not empathic to Rose as a person. She was not ready to hear it so starkly. That doesn't mean that she was in denial, I don't think she ever was, but she had not been involved in exploring the consequences of her illness and she had known this doctor for about 15 minutes.

Why do we, as doctors, feel that we have to tell a patient everything as soon as possible? Teaching has switched from the paternalistic attitude of not telling our patients anything to telling them everything 'for their own good'. Does it make us feel better to get this bad news 'out there'? Why can we not be led at a pace that suits our patients? Doctors, in general, believe that patients should know the truth

---

[8] I am referring to Elizabeth Kubler Ross and David Kessler. On Grief and Grieving: Finding the Meaning of Grief through the Five Stages of Loss. Simon & Schuster 2005. There have been many disputes over and developments of the ideas in this book, but most people still refer to the five stages. Anger is the second stage. Denial, Anger, Bargaining, Depression and Acceptance are the five stages.

in order for us to have a 'partnership'. This is the same philosophy again really, that 'doctor knows best', but in this version, patients should know the truth rather than be protected from it. I remember when I was at medical school, a close friend of mine had metastatic breast cancer (that is, cancer that had spread and was therefore incurable). She always refused to acknowledge it and would never allow anyone to talk about it with her. I felt she was selfish and misguided as we all needed to grieve and have the ability to talk about our past life episodes together. Of course, it wasn't selfish of her but of me. One thing I have tried to live by as a doctor is that it is not about us. It is about the patient. We must accept our patient's way of dealing with things rather than stick to some script we have been taught. Of course, we can gently probe and offer silence to our patients to allow them to talk if they want to but are having trouble doing so. This is wonderfully brought out in the book by Kathryn Mannix, mentioned above, a palliative care consultant. She tells the story of a young woman who is dying of metastatic melanoma but she only talks about the number of children she is going to have and her plans for the future. This is very distressing for her family who feel they cannot say a proper goodbye to her. After the consultant takes the family away to discuss this, they come up with a plan whereby they can help their daughter and wife by not challenging her but by saying things they want to say without implying that these are goodbyes. It seemed to work and the young woman died peacefully a few days later without having to openly confront her own death. This seemed the right thing for this patient even if it makes us, as medics, feel uncomfortable.

Unfortunately, Rose did not manage to forge a relationship with this consultant until she was nearing the end of her illness when she 'forgave' her and, perhaps, understood her approach better. I remember vividly that about three months into her illness, when she was indeed very unwell, she told me she would die the following week because that was what the consultant had said – she had picked up the three months part of the prognosis given to her. It broke my heart that that was what she had taken from the consultation and it had been in her mind all that time. Paul Kalanithi addresses this in his book when talking about how he approached the issue with patients:

> "It is important to be accurate, but you must always
> leave room for hope ... the problem is you can't tell a

patient where she sits on the (survival) curve: Will she die in six months or sixty? I came to believe that it is irresponsible to be more precise than you can be accurate. Those apocryphal doctors who gave specific numbers: Who were they, I wondered, and who taught them statistics?"[9]

Interestingly, when he was first diagnosed, he had an exchange with his oncologist:
"I know now is not the time, but I want to talk about the Kaplan-Meier survival curves."
"No," she said, "absolutely not!"[10]

This is the issue we face – everything may be plain in theory, but we are dealing with individual people who may not be able to behave in line with the theory, even if they themselves believe in it.

Clinicians often make comments that can have profound, unintentionally devastating, effects on the listener. Even throw-away remarks can cause hurt and anxiety that we are not aware of. I do remember one of my patients making a complaint about me being 'flippant', when I thought I was just trying to lighten her mood with my repartee. This did make me more conscious of what I say. As human beings, not just doctors, we should reflect on the effects of our words and behaviour.

At this time, when Rose was trying to assimilate the consequences of her illness, she also had a clinic appointment to see the Respiratory Consultant who saw all the patients with mesothelioma in the Oxfordshire area and followed them through their illness. Rose was only 33 and the majority of his patients would have been 60 or more. He was a study in how to communicate difficult things. I sat in the room as before, but he put the chair for me in a part of the room that was out of his line of vision when talking to Rose, and also out of her line of vision. He asked her about what the worst things were about her illness and waited until she responded with something before speaking again. He

---

[9] Paul Kalanithi Ibid P 95
[10] Ibid P122

managed to get her to say all the things she missed being able to do and to express some of her fears and her sadness. She asked him what proportion of people with a diagnosis of mesothelioma opted for chemotherapy, given that it wasn't curative but may extend life. He answered her honestly (about 60%) and understood her decision to try it given her young age. He was patient and gentle. Rose thought he was lovely and wanted to go back and see him, despite the huge effort it was for her to get to the clinic appointments, even though she knew he could not 'do anything' for her.

The only thing that might have been offered to her was an operation to remove the peritoneum (the lining of the abdomen). This is a huge operation, again not curative, and is only done in a couple of centres in the UK. All her results and scans were sent to Basingstoke where they have Multi-Disciplinary Team (MDT) meetings of all cases of mesothelioma in the south of England and discuss the option of surgery in each case. For Rose, it was decided that her disease was too far advanced. I'm not sure what Rose thought of this but I had mixed emotions. Again, it comes down to the balance of hope versus reality, and an operation that would take weeks to recover from, perhaps for no reason, giving false hope. But on the other hand, I wanted my daughter to have a longer life as she had so many things to do. The MDT did say, though, that if six months of chemotherapy had shrunk the tumours enough then they would reconsider. And so, we moved onto the next phase.

Looking back on this time I find it hard to believe how our lives can change so abruptly and so quickly. I know that this is the case when someone loses a loved one through accident or sudden death, but this was like being in an endless dream, a nightmare. I still do not understand how Rose kept herself together during that summer and autumn; how she, at least for a while, maintained her sense of humour and her ability to entertain all those who came to see her. That was the old Rose struggling with her new circumstances and managing to overcome them whilst her friends were around. But it didn't last long.

CHAPTER 3
Palliative treatment

Rose opted to have six rounds of chemotherapy in the full knowledge that it was not a cure. Due to the possibility of the operation, it was agreed that she have three rounds and then another CT scan to see if the tumour had responded. The chemotherapy took place in the day treatment unit of the John Radcliffe Hospital (JR). It was a pleasant enough environment and the first chemotherapy took all day as the nurses have to be careful about any reactions to the medication. I sat with her all day, which I was to do on many occasions when she was in hospital or the hospice. I found it an interesting experience, to see everything that went on all day (and once or twice all night) from a different point of view. It made me reflect on how I had behaved to patients when I walked the wards during the early part of my career. Most of the time it was just boring.

Two days after the chemotherapy Rose started vomiting. Of course, this is normal, and she had been given drugs to try to lessen the effects. She tried all sorts of pills but nothing worked. After a week, I took her to the Oncology Triage Unit in the JR so they could rehydrate her and try different pills or injections. I felt that the pills were not working partly due to the nature of her disease: it was obvious to me, illustrated by her low haemoglobin and low albumin (protein) in her blood, that she wasn't absorbing anything through the stomach, so perhaps she wasn't absorbing the pills either? The fluids they gave her and the injection did help and she was sent home with more pills.

However, she continued to vomit about three to five times every day. I was concerned about her hydration and I called the triage ward. I did not know the system: as it was the middle of the night and the triage ward was closed, a triage nurse from the oncology ward spoke to me. He said it was difficult because the oncology team did not admit people during the night and that I should take her to Accident and Emergency. To me, that was completely inappropriate. I am fully aware of what would happen in A&E – it's fantastic for medical and surgical emergencies but not good for sick patients with chronic disease. I'm sure she wouldn't have gone anyway: throughout her illness and increasingly as time went on, she would not easily agree to go to hospital. So, I took a deep breath and called 111. My deep breath? My last job in Cambridge had been as Medical Director of the Out-of-Hours service which was doctor-led and only accessible through 111. I knew all about 111! It did not disappoint. After asking me the usual mostly irrelevant questions the non-clinical person had to go through, they arrived at a 'disposition'. For Rose, this was 'talk to a doctor within six hours'. I said I wanted to speak to a doctor straight away: her response was 'are you refusing the disposition' – making me into the bad guy! I don't blame her; the 111 system does not allow for common sense or any diversion from the 'one size fits all' model. Anyway, I told her I was refusing it because I wanted to speak to a GP as soon as possible. To be fair (and this is down to the Out-of-Hours service rather than 111), a doctor rang me back fairly quickly and came out straight away to give Rose an injection. Again, I am someone who knows the system and was able to get the appropriate care, but what of the ordinary person with no clinical knowledge? No wonder there is such frustration outside normal GP hours.

Rose had the second round of chemotherapy and was vomiting throughout it. Afterwards, things got even worse and she was eating very little. Her haemoglobin had dropped again and she went back to the triage unit for another transfusion and more injections. She had a syringe driver set up with an antiemetic (anti sickness drug). This is a pump that runs over 24 hrs delivering medications through a small needle under the skin. It revolutionised palliative care as people did not have to have injections all the time. The drug is delivered to maintain a steady level in the bloodstream and patients who are able can walk around with them. Rose had to be admitted overnight as the unit closed at 8 p.m. and the blood transfusion wasn't finished. No beds were available on the oncology ward so she was sent to the gastrointestinal ward, where there were patients having endoscopies and biopsies and other treatments and investigations for the stomach and upper gastrointestinal tract. They did not know anything about Rose. When she vomited, she was asked, by a well-meaning nurse no doubt, if she wanted something for the sickness! They also did not seem to understand the syringe driver. The following day the doctor did not come and see her until 5 p.m. so she was waiting to go home all day, and still vomiting. The doctor, when she did come, rather unhelpfully said that Rose should stay in until she stopped vomiting. Rose, normally not one to challenge doctors or those in authority, muttered something along the lines of "well, I'll be here for a few weeks then." I took her home, against the advice.

After another couple of weeks Rose was still vomiting several times a day, not eating much and getting very weak. She had been referred to the palliative care team by now, a bit of a feat really because they wanted her to be under the oncologists as she was still having treatment. I said that the 'treatment' was palliative and therefore she should be under their team. I was in discussion with them, trying to get her admitted to the hospice for symptom control. They agreed to discuss her in the morning meeting the following day and agree her priority for a bed. The next morning, I was on the phone to the hospice senior nurse whilst the district nurse, who was unfortunately one we had not met before as she was covering absence, was seeing Rose. She did not know Rose or me and did not seem to have a grip on the case. As part of her cancer, Rose had had fevers and sweats and her blood pressure had been consistently low. After talking it through with Rose we had decided not to take her temperature anymore as it made her anxious if it was high, especially during the chemotherapy. The district nurse had thought her sleepy and had taken her temperature and her blood pressure. I was on the phone and the hospice had just said they would have a bed for Rose that day. The district nurse came into the room and, realising who I was speaking to, asked to speak to them. I handed over my phone and she proceeded to tell the nurse on the phone how concerned she was as Rose had a significant fever, low blood pressure and a fast pulse, and scored her high on the sepsis scale (Sepsis is an infection that affects the whole body and from which people can die very rapidly. It is now the subject of much training of medical professionals.). I couldn't believe my ears – I knew the hospice wouldn't take her if they thought she was septic, and I knew that Rose would refuse to go back into hospital. I grabbed my phone, rather rudely, and tried to calmly tell the hospice nurse that in my opinion Rose wasn't septic as she was no different than she had been in the past. I also told him that she would refuse to go back into the JR. I tried subtly to tell him that this district nurse did not know Rose and that although 'doing her job', was not clued up to the situation. I did not want to undermine the district nurse but I was desperate that Rose got to the hospice. He said he would discuss it with the doctor and call me back. To his credit, he did so very quickly and offered the bed, understanding, I think, my underlying message.

I was very disappointed with the district nurse, not for doing the observations, but for giving the palliative nurse her assessment of what should happen without discussing it with me, or more importantly, with Rose. I understand she was following protocol but she had no idea about Rose's wishes. I always try to instil it in my GP trainees that there is no point in arranging admission of a patient to hospital until they have discussed this course of action with them and found out their wishes. In extreme cases you may have to accept their wishes not to be admitted, against your better judgement, as long as the patient has 'capacity' (that is, has the mental capacity to make that decision). I had once encountered such a situation whilst out with my trainee on a home visit where a patient refused firstly to get in the ambulance that had been called and then refused again to go to hospital when we had been brought in to 'persuade her'. I told her she might die if she did not go to hospital; she understood this and still refused. That is her prerogative. That this district nurse had not even discussed it with Rose was, in my view, verging on the unprofessional. Again, if I had not intervened, had not had the medical knowledge and confidence to say that Rose was not septic, she would probably have ended up in A&E, or stayed at home and got worse through her dehydration. Although I seem to be criticising this district nurse, I understand that her position was difficult. In general, the district nurses were absolutely fantastic and were often there for me as well as for Rose.

When Rose got to the hospice, she was given strong IV antibiotics to be on the safe side. Her blood tests came back showing she was unlikely to have an infection, but was still anaemic, the last transfusion having had no effect at all on her haemoglobin which was a bit of a worry. The consultant at the hospice was brilliant, as were all the staff there. I tentatively suggested that Rose probably didn't have an infection, and he agreed and the antibiotics were stopped. Rose had another blood transfusion. I was impressed by the amount of time that the doctors and nurses spent with the patients in the hospice and the consultant was very gentle with Rose. I remember he said then, and later when he got to know her a bit better, "You are an intelligent person who I am sure understands exactly what your illness means, but that you don't really want to talk about that, am I right?"' So, finally, someone who was honest yet allowed Rose to dictate what she wanted to know and talk about (along with the respiratory consultant).

The vomiting, however, did not stop despite her being on a syringe driver. Rose stopped eating. She had hardly eaten anything since the chemotherapy started and for the next three weeks, she ate absolutely nothing. I was watching my daughter starve to death. Despite not eating she was still vomiting, fluid and bile. She wouldn't go out, she often pretended to be asleep when her friends came around as she was too exhausted to engage with them.

Rose told me that she couldn't really face any more chemotherapy but was frightened of stopping. We saw the oncologist and after some discussion, a joint decision was made that she shouldn't have any more chemotherapy. Rose also decided not to have the CT scan to check any change in the tumour load. She had had two rounds of chemotherapy so it was unlikely to have had any positive effect, and I don't think Rose wanted to see the evidence of a lack of progress after suffering so much from it. So that was the end of any attempt to extend Rose's life.

CHAPTER 4

A brief look at asbestos

No link could be proven between Rose's mesothelioma and asbestos exposure. I racked my brains about places she may have been exposed, and my instinct was, and is, that she may have been exposed whilst in Argentina as an 18-year-old where she was helping build a school. I have a lovely picture of her, now rather poignant, brandishing a trowel beside a wall she was building. This building site may have been on the site of previous buildings that contains asbestos. I have no proof but it prompted me to try to find out more about the industry.

There has been a lot of research about asbestos, and its health risks are indisputable. Much of this information, however, is not widely publicised or known. The International Ban Asbestos Secretariat (IBAS) has produced many papers on the world-wide situation along with evidence of the effects of contact with asbestos. The following extracts I have picked out as being helpful to understanding the risk of asbestos and its current status in the world. A visit to the website will give interested readers much more information.[11]

Firstly, given the evidence about asbestos as a cause of several types of cancer, mesothelioma being the main one, I had expected it to have been banned throughout the world, at the least in the developed world. The following is the most up-to-date list I could find of countries which have banned the import, production and use of asbestos.

---

[11] http://www.ibasecretariat.org/

National Asbestos Bans[12]:

Algeria	Denmark	Ireland	Monaco	Slovakia
Argentina	Djibouti	Israel	Mozambique	Slovenia
Australia	Egypt	Italy	Netherlands	South Africa
Austria	Estonia	Japan	New Caledonia	Spain
Bahrain	Finland	Jordan	New Zealand	Sweden
Belgium	France	Korea (South)	Norway	Switzerland
Brazil	Gabon	Kuwait	Oman	Taiwan
Brunei	Germany	Latvia	Poland	Turkey
Bulgaria	Gibraltar	Liechtenstein	Portugal	United Kingdom
Canada	Greece	Lithuania	Qatar	Uruguay
Chile	Honduras	Luxembourg	Romania	
Croatia	Hungary	Macedonia	Saudi Arabia	
Cyprus	Iceland	Malta	Serbia	
Czech Republic	Iraq	Mauritius	Seychelles	

It is surprising to me, and no doubt to my readers, that the USA is not included in this list. They have strict rules as to the use of asbestos, but it is not banned in the USA.

---

[12] Exemptions for minor uses are permitted in some countries listed; however, all countries listed must have banned the use of all types of asbestos. Additionally, we seek to ensure that all general use of asbestos, i.e. in construction, insulation, textiles, etc., has been expressly prohibited. The exemptions usually encountered are for specialist seals and gaskets; in a few countries there is an interim period where asbestos brake pads are permitted. International Ban Asbestos Secretariat. (http://ibasecretariat.org/)

In terms of the main producers, the following list gives us the top five[13]:

World Mine Production and Reserves (tons)

Country	2019	2020	Reserves
United States	-	-	Small
Brazil	15,000	60,000	11,000
China	150,000	100,000	95,000
Kazakhstan	211,000	210,000	Large
Russia	790,000	790,000	110,000,000
Zimbabwe	2,500	8000	Large
World (total)	1,170,000	1,200,000	Large

A further article by Laurie Kazan-Allen [14]in the IBAS gives us much more information. In her article she demonstrates the occupational and environmental exposure that people still face throughout the world. Occupationally, it affects workers at all stages of the process of the extraction, transportation and use of asbestos. The highest incidence of asbestos-related disease seems to be amongst those working in heavy industries such as shipbuilding, railway engineering and the insulation industry (and those who washed their clothes).

Builders and DIY enthusiasts have also been exposed, and there are many asbestos materials used in public buildings such as schools and hospitals.

The World Health Organization estimates that today 125 million people are being occupationally exposed to asbestos and that such exposure leads to 90,000 deaths every year; the ILO believes that 100,000 people die annually from workplace asbestos exposures.

There is also evidence of exposure environmentally. Many examples are things that we would not automatically link with asbestos. For example, the attack on the World Trade Centre liberated 5,000 tonnes of asbestos from fireproofing and floor tiles used in the twin

---

[13] https://pubs.usgs.gov/periodicals/mcs2021/mcs2021.pdf
[14] Asbestos Exposure. Laurie Kazan-Allen IBAS 2018
http://ibasecretariat.org/prof_asb_exposure.php

towers. In the aftermath of the 2004 tsunami, the coastline of Sri Lanka was strewn with asbestos debris. Similarly, after the Japan earthquake and tsunami of 2011, the majority of debris collected in the Sendai area in April 2011 confirmed the presence of asbestos contamination.

At least 107,000 people die each year world-wide from asbestos-related lung cancer, mesothelioma and asbestosis resulting from occupational exposures. However, known exposure cannot always be traced and in Britain the risk has been estimated:

> The risk of mesothelioma for the rest of the UK population who haven't experienced (these) occupational exposures is about one in 1000. These apparently unexposed cases account for 60 per cent of all mesotheliomas in women and 15 per cent in men. This is higher than the overall rate in women in most other countries, suggesting that many of these unexplained cases were caused by unrecognised environmental asbestos exposures which occurred in certain situations because of the widespread use of asbestos during the 1960s and 1970s.[15]

There is a long lead time for the disease (ie the number of years between exposure and diagnosis). Even if a country has banned asbestos, there will still be a lot in old structures. The problem is not going away.

> Even in the countries which have banned the use of all new asbestos, a large body of asbestos and asbestos-containing materials do still exist in the facilities, structures, industrial settings, buildings, vehicles and in many other locations. Many countries have emphasised the importance of making risk-based decisions about whether asbestos currently in buildings should be removed (with attendant risks to those doing this work, and possibly others) or managed by safe methods of retention (in which the potential release of fibres is minimised). It is important

---

[15] http://www.hse.gov.uk/research/rrhtm/rr696.htm

to carefully protect workers' health in the demolition and other works from a potential exposure to existing asbestos. Adequate measures should also be instituted for protection of the health of population and environment in the handling and disposal of asbestos waste and asbestos containing materials. There should be systematic surveys of the existing asbestos in various settings, and proper labelling, information and guidance should be provided for appropriate behaviour and actions in such environments.[16]

Further, the WHO outline recommendations:

Bearing in mind that there is no evidence for a threshold for the carcinogenic effect of asbestos, including chrysotile, and that increased cancer risks have been observed in populations exposed to very low levels, the most efficient way to eliminate asbestos-related diseases is to stop using all types of asbestos. Continued use of asbestos cement in the construction industry is a particular concern, because the workforce is large, it is difficult to control exposure, and in-place materials have the potential to deteriorate and pose a risk to those carrying out alterations, maintenance and demolition. In its various applications, asbestos can be replaced by some fibre materials and by other products that pose less or no risk to health.

Materials containing asbestos should be encapsulated, and, in general, it is not recommended to carry out work that is likely to disturb asbestos fibres. If necessary, such work should be carried out only under strict control measures to avoid exposure to asbestos,

---

[16] WHO: National Programmes for the Elimination of asbestos-related diseases. https://www.who.int/occupational_health/publications/asbestosdoc/en/

such as encapsulation, wet processes, local exhaust ventilation with filtration, and regular cleaning. It also requires the use of personal protective equipment – special respirators, safety goggles, protective gloves and clothing – and the provision of special facilities for their decontamination.

WHO is committed to working with countries towards the elimination of asbestos-related diseases in the following strategic directions:

by recognizing that the most efficient way to eliminate asbestos-related diseases is to stop the use of all types of asbestos;

by providing information about solutions for replacing asbestos with safer substitutes and developing economic and technological mechanisms to stimulate its replacement;

by taking measures to prevent exposure to asbestos in place and during asbestos removal (abatement);

by improving early diagnosis, treatment and rehabilitation services for asbestos-related diseases and establishing registries of people with past and/or current exposure to asbestos.

WHO strongly recommends planning for and implementing these measures as part of a comprehensive national approach for the elimination of asbestos-related diseases. Such an approach should also include developing national profiles, awareness raising, capacity building, an institutional framework and a national plan of action for the elimination of asbestos-related diseases.

WHO will collaborate with ILO on implementation of the Resolution concerning asbestos, adopted by the Ninety-fifth Session of the International Labour Conference (16), and will work with other intergovernmental organizations and civil society towards the elimination of asbestos-related diseases worldwide. [17]

In the UK there has been evidence of schoolteachers and students from specific schools having contracted mesothelioma and there is a continuing campaign for the safe removal of all asbestos from schools. I remember that Rose told me that they were removing asbestos from her halls of residence in Newcastle when she lived there in her first year of university.

The list of occupations where cases of mesothelioma has been identified tells us that although there are significantly more cases in risky occupations like carpentry, shipbuilding, plumbing and construction work, there are also cases amongst farmers, butchers, textile workers and even lawyers and doctors.

Of course, I was interested in the situation in Argentina. This is an extract from the IBAS.

> Argentina has banned asbestos! The final resolution, signed on July 26, 2001 became law on July 31 when it was published in the Official Bulletin. Resolution 823/01 stipulates that the use of chrysotile in textiles, paper, rubber, plastic, paint and insulating products, filters and gaskets will be prohibited sixty days after publication. The import, trade and uses of chrysotile which remain legal will be strictly regulated until January 1, 2003 when they too are banned ....
>
> The first limitations on the use of asbestos in Argentina began in 1979 with the enactment of the implementing Decree of Law 19,587 on Industrial Hygiene and Safety. More than twenty years later Resolutions No.845/00 and No.823/01 of the Federal Ministry of Health finally prohibited the use of asbestos.

---

[17] WHO Recommendations on prevention of asbestos-related diseases. https://www.who.int/ipcs/assessment/public_health/Elimination_asbestos-related_diseases_EN.pdf

Waste containing asbestos is considered hazardous waste, and so the provisions of Law 24,051, relating to hazardous waste in general, apply.

Main obligations

The demolition or repair of structures or buildings containing asbestos can only be performed in compliance with the relevant regulations.

Permits and regulator

The control of the presence of asbestos is under the area of the Ministry of Health. However, labour obligations also contain specific provisions relating to air pollution, quality of workplace, and so on.

Penalties

There are no specific environmental sanctions on the improper use or handling of asbestos[18]

Asbestos is still being mined, produced and used in several countries, including those with the largest populations – India and China. Regulations about its use are varied. The interesting and informative article by Laurie Kazan Allen above gives us an almost limitless view of how populations are exposed to asbestos. Whilst in the developed countries we are seeing a slight fall in cases of mesothelioma, there is predicted to be a large disease burden in developing countries unless strict regulation and bans are introduced soon.

Exposure to asbestos does not necessarily mean that a person will develop mesothelioma. There are many other factors involved. I have looked at this in more detail in the chapter on mesothelioma. As an introduction to that chapter, I will put it in context. As a GP, I had never heard of mesothelioma outside the pleural (lung) cavity, and therefore would not have thought of it myself. I hope I would have taken seriously someone who rarely visits the doctor and had the symptoms Rose had. However, many people present earlier with vaguer symptoms and no signs. This is a plea to GPs, therefore, to have this disease on their radar.

As I said, I had never heard of peritoneal mesothelioma. Of course, I had heard of mesothelioma and knew that it was basically a

---

[18] Frederico S. Deyá, Marval, O'Farrell & Mairal: Environmental Law and practice in Argentina. www.practicallaw.com/environment-mjg

death sentence. Thus, when I heard the term first used about Rose my mind just stopped. I knew from my training that this happens to patients when they are told something that is bad news. I had observed it when accompanying patients to clinic when I was training and I was aware in my own patients that they may only pick up about 10% of what is said: hence, the encouragement to take someone with them to consultations. Now I was experiencing it first hand. Rose was adamant that she did not want people to look up the diagnosis and insisted that she would not either. Of course, other people who loved her did not want to go against her wishes, but they felt they needed to know about the illness. So, my son David, ever the academic, looked up all the academic articles he could find, and with his non-medical brain quickly understood that this was not a good diagnosis to have. Similarly, I felt that I needed to know as much as possible because I needed to know the options that were being offered her were based in good research evidence.

So, what is peritoneal mesothelioma and how does it behave? In the UK there are around 2,700 new cases of mesothelioma per year. The proportion that are in the peritoneum varies from study to study from around 3% to 10%. Thus, this is a rare disease. Women appear to develop peritoneal mesothelioma disproportionately to men, when compared to mesothelioma as a whole. The reason for this is not clear.

CHAPTER 5
What is peritoneal mesothelioma?

<u>Causes</u>

Malignant mesothelioma (MM) has been shown to be linked to asbestos exposure; other mineralogical and environmental factors also contribute to MM susceptibility. Over 80% of MM patients have a known history of asbestos exposure. Asbestos refers to a family of six mineral fibres and is classified into two subgroups: (i) the amphiboles, a group of rod-like fibres including amosite (brown asbestos), crocidolite (blue asbestos), anthophyllite, actinolite and tremolite; and (ii) the serpentine group, consisting of chrysotile (white asbestos). The association between amphibole asbestos exposure and MM development is well known. In particular, crocidolite is considered to be the most carcinogenic type of asbestos. Erionite, an asbestos-like mineral, also causes MM.

However, fewer than 5% of asbestos workers develop MM, which suggests that people have different genetic susceptibilities to MM development. For instance, genetic background has been indicated to have a role in determining susceptibility to mineral fibre carcinogenesis, specifically to erionite.[19]

Having said this, although 20% of cases, according to this article, cannot be linked directly with asbestos exposure, it is assumed that there has been some at some time in a cancer patient's life.

In terms of peritoneal mesothelioma, it is thought that the fibres are ingested, but it can also be caused through the spread of inhaled asbestos through the lymph system. Whether the exposure is known or not, it can take anything from 15 to 60 years for the cancer to develop.

<u>Symptoms</u>

As said above, women are increasingly likely to develop peritoneal mesothelioma and it often takes a long time to be diagnosed because of the vagueness of the symptoms and the traditional view that mesothelioma is a male disease linked to the workplace.

---

[19] Yoshitaka Sekido: Molecular Pathogenesis of Malignant Mesothelioma. Carcinogenesis, Vol 34, Issue 7, July 2013 P1413-1419

Symptoms include abdominal pain or swelling, weight loss, loss of appetite, diarrhoea or constipation, night sweats, fever and fatigue. Rose did not have any pain and her bowels were working normally. However, she scored positive for all the other symptoms. Obviously, there are other causes of these symptoms, not all malignant, and I am grateful to the GP trainee who sent her straight to the hospital to get bloods and X-rays done. The advice to doctors is summed up in the American Journal of Medicine

> In summary, for the patient with nonspecific abdominal symptoms, a thorough history should include assessment for potential exposure risks including asbestos, therapeutic radiation, or chronic peritoneal irritation. Any of these should prompt the addition of peritoneal mesothelioma to the differential diagnosis. Yet history alone may not be enough to trigger consideration, and we argue that the possibility of malignant peritoneal mesothelioma should be contemplated in any patient reporting significant prolonged symptoms without a previous definitive diagnosis. A CT scan should be obtained, and if concern for malignant disease is present, tissue sampling is essential. Laparoscopic biopsy is the gold standard, and often the only option, for obtaining diagnostic tissue. Persistent diagnostic efforts will facilitate earlier discussions about initiation of aggressive treatment vs palliative care[20]

Types and stages
There are three types of mesothelioma:
Epithelioid mesotheliomas are the most common and respond best to treatment. Up to 75% of mesotheliomas are epithelioid.
Sarcomatoid cells are the least common, at around 10%, and respond poorly to treatment.

---

[20] Bet s Zha, Margaret Flanagan, Caley Coulson, Kanishka W Garvin: Difficult to Identify: Malignant Primary Peritoneal Mesothelioma. American Journal of Medicine, Vol 128, Issue11, Nov 2015 P1191-1194

Biphasic tumours are made of epithelial and sarcomatoid cells. The response of biphasic mesothelioma to treatment depends on the ratio of epithelioid to sarcomatoid cells.

There are four stages of peritoneal mesothelioma, although staging is not as precise as it is with other cancers.

Stage 1

Cancerous tissue is minimal, tumours are contained within the abdominal lining, and lymph nodes are free of cancer.

Stage 2

Cancerous tissue is moderate and tumours have not spread outside the lining or to lymph nodes.

Stage 3

Cancerous tissue is more extensive and tumours may have spread outside the peritoneal lining, to lymph nodes or both.

It is generally accepted that patients with extensive tumour spreading are classified as stage IV.

Diagnosis

As indicated above, definitive diagnosis is through histological examination of tissue biopsied from the peritoneum. Other examinations can give clues to the diagnosis, for example, blood tests, chest and abdominal X-rays and CT scans. In Rose's case, her blood tests at presentation were grossly abnormal, her chest X-ray showed pericardial and pleural effusions and her CT scan showed ascites (fluid in the abdomen) and a thickening of the peritoneum.

Her blood tests showed a significant anaemia (Hb of 70) high inflammatory markers (a CRP of nearly 300), a significant thrombocytosis (high platelet count of 946) and severe hypoalbuminaemia (low albumin or protein of 13). Even though Rose was working, doing social things, exercising and basically living a normal life (albeit feeling very tired and seen to fall asleep at her desk), she presented with such abnormal results that it was hard for the doctors to believe she had been functioning at all. Being young, her body was able to compensate, a good thing in one way but unfortunately it meant that she presented with advanced disease.

Diagnosis can result from examination of the pleural or peritoneal fluid, but histology of biopsies is gold standard. Rose had a laparoscopy when she had been passed as fit enough by the medics and cardiologists – they were concerned about her blood results and her pericardial effusion. The nature of the results and how they were communicated to her is detailed elsewhere in the book.

Treatment

No treatment is curative. However, life expectancy can be increased with some treatments. The basic treatment is chemotherapy, using cisplatin and pemetrexed. Rose was offered six cycles of this and then she would have another CT scan. Her results had all been sent to Basingstoke, one of two specialist centres in the country who offered surgery. She was not deemed suitable for surgery but would be reconsidered at their MDT meeting after the chemotherapy. The most effective treatment so far is cytoreductive surgery combined with heated intraperitoneal chemotherapy (HIPEC). This is performed on a case-by-case basis and has been shown in small studies to extend survival and improve quality of life. However, it is only offered to patients who are physically fit to be able to withstand the 10-hour operation, and to those where the disease is in the early stages. Radiotherapy can also be offered palliatively.

There are few clinical trials for mesothelioma, the majority being for pleural mesothelioma. They explore the use of biologicals and of gene therapy. In the former, the new biological drugs are combined with chemotherapy. Rose was not considered eligible for these trials, partly because it became clear she could not tolerate the chemotherapy.

Prognosis

There is no cure for peritoneal mesothelioma. Treatments can extend life and offer an improved quality of life. The median survival of untreated peritoneal mesothelioma is six months. The average five-year survival rate for all patients is 9%. Age is a strong factor, but this is mainly because younger patients can tolerate stronger treatments. In Rose's case, she had two rounds of chemotherapy and could not tolerate any more – in fact the chemotherapy itself nearly killed her.

In terms of prognostic factors, obviously the stage of disease at presentation is crucial. There has been an interesting study which points to two independent adverse prognostic factors:

Serum albumin (ALB) can indicate the nutritional status, which is an independent prognostic factor for many cancers, including pancreatic carcinoma, gastric carcinoma, nasopharyngeal carcinoma, bladder cancer, and malignant pleural mesothelioma.

The blood neutrophil-to-lymphocyte ratio (NLR) is systemic markers of inflammation. Strong evidence suggests that the NLR can be used to indicate the inflammation condition. Previous studies have shown that NLR is an independent prognostic factor for many cancers, such as colorectal cancer, breast cancer, soft tissue sarcoma, and bladder cancer.

The Cox proportional regression analysis showed that a NLR $\geq$ 3 was an independent adverse prognostic factor for MPeM (Malignant Peritoneal Mesothelioma).

The Cox proportional regression analysis showed that hypoalbuminemia (low albumin) was an independent adverse prognostic factor for MPeM.

NLR and ALB are simple, inexpensive, and commonly performed laboratory tests. Blood cell analysis and hepatic functions are routine exams. ALB is measured as a part of the hepatic function tests, and the NLR is defined as the absolute neutrophil count divided by the absolute lymphocyte count. Therefore, I stress that the potential prognostic roles of ALB and NLR in MPeM are important.[21]

I do not know what Rose's NLR was, though if it was an indication of inflammation, her inflammatory marker, CRP, was very

---

[21] Wenjie Yin, Guoqi Zheng, KunnaYung, Hui Song, Yufrei Liang: Analysis of prognostic factors of patients with malignant peritoneal mesothelioma. World J Surg Oncol 2018; 16:44. Published online 2018 March 5 0.1186/s12957-018-1350-5 PMCID:PMC5836427

high. Certainly, her albumin was extremely low (the doctors commented that they had never seen such a low albumin).

Thus, this pernicious cancer is hard to diagnose, difficult even to have in mind when seeing yet another person with vague symptoms. Although I personally think we over-investigate people with X-rays and scans, I am a great believer in blood tests showing abnormalities at even early stages of disease. Certainly, if Rose had had those blood tests done three months earlier, I believe they would have shown abnormalities that could have been followed up. If she had had abdominal pain, she may have presented earlier. It is a lesson to all us GPs to keep an open mind and to 'think outside the box'.

Research

Research on malignant mesothelioma is not abundant, probably because it is a rare cancer. However, as it is one that cannot be cured, there is increasing interest in research in this area as more and more cancers are treatable.

A study was carried out in ACT (basically, Canberra) in Australia where properties were identified in which asbestos insulation had been fitted. Interestingly, we had lived in a house in Canberra when Rose was nine months old.

> We observed an incidence of mesothelioma around two and a half times higher in males who had ever lived in ACT houses containing loose-fill asbestos insulation (affected residential properties) than in males who had not. Of the other six cancers known to be associated or potentially associated with asbestos exposure, only colorectal cancer incidence was significantly elevated in residents who had lived at an affected property (exposed) compared with those who had not (unexposed).
>
> Our observation of an elevated SIR for mesothelioma in men but not women is consistent with previous evidence. This finding could suggest confounding by occupational exposure to asbestos, but it is unlikely that such exposure would be distributed differentially among residents who had and had not lived at an affected property. The association could indicate

higher levels of exposure to loose-fill insulation among men. In a survey of residents of affected residential properties, a higher proportion of men than women reported entering the roof space (85% vs 41%), and 15% of men who had reported entering the roof space did so more than 50 times.[22]

The National Centre for Mesothelioma Research at Imperial College is one centre where research is being done and co-ordinated. They are concentrating on the genomic basis as there is some evidence that one's genetic makeup could affect the risk of mesothelioma: not all people exposed to the same level of the same asbestos develop mesothelioma in their lifetime. Another example comes from a study in Turkey on erionite, another cause of mesothelioma. They found that all members of some families exposed to erionite developed mesothelioma whereas no members of other families exposed to erionite developed it.

Understanding changes in the genes of the mesothelioma cells helps in developing treatments. They aim to understand more about how mesothelioma develops and how gene changes in cancer cells affect how well different treatments work.

Several gene mutations have been identified and found in patients with mesothelioma. These include NF2 and BAP-1.

Gene mutation testing is not performed routinely in mesothelioma. It may sometimes be performed as part of a clinical trial.

Studies of cancers are often limited by the availability of tissue for research as, until recently, genetic sequencing has required relatively large tissue samples gained by a surgical procedure. Unfortunately, most patients with mesothelioma and lung cancer present late in the disease when they are too unwell for this surgery. For this reason, genetic investigations into lung cancer and mesothelioma have been carried out on the minority of patients with mild or moderate disease, and the results may be biased. In addition, solid tumours are complex mixtures of cells including non-cancerous fibroblasts, endothelial cells, lymphocytes, and

---

[22] Korda, Clements, Armstrong, Hsei, Tenniel, Anderson et al. Risk of Cancer associated with residential exposure to asbestos insulation: a whole-population cohort study. The Lancet, Nov 1 2017 pp 522-528

macrophages that often contribute more than 50% of the total DNA or RNA extracted. This can make the molecular classification of these tumours difficult. Genome analysis of bulk surgical specimens may also miss important mutations that are present only in a subset of cells, or in certain sites.

Immunotherapy is also a direction that research is taking. There was a large trial using tremelimumab. The DETERMINE study investigated the effects of the cytotoxic-T-lymphocyte-associated antigen 4 (CTLA-4) monoclonal antibody tremelimumab in patients with previously treated advanced malignant mesothelioma. DETERMINE was a double-blind, placebo-controlled, phase 2b trial done at 105 study centres across 19 countries in patients with unresectable pleural or peritoneal malignant mesothelioma who had progressed after one or two previous systemic treatments for advanced disease. 2,014, 571 patients took part in the trial.

The results of this trial were that tremelimumab did not significantly prolong overall survival compared with placebo in patients with previously treated malignant mesothelioma. [23]

Whilst the results of this trial are disappointing, it has been stated that:

> It is unlikely that in a complex solid tumour such as mesothelioma, a single immunotherapy can show survival benefit.[24]

I did not put together this chapter on research during the time I was looking after Rose. However, I did enough reading to know that there was little, if anything, that could be done for her: We might have been able to extend her life by a few weeks if she had completed the chemotherapy, but there was no possibility of a cure. David, having done his research, also came to this conclusion. Bob, I think, did not want to think about it and therefore did not want to know – very unusual for him who always wanted to know about everything he came across. I did at

---

[23] The Lancet Sept 2017 p1137-1284

[24] Prasad S. Adusumilli (Memorial Sloan Kettering Cancer Center, New York, NY, USA) The Lancet July 2016

one point, as I've explained, begin to feel that I had not explored the possibilities enough and that somehow I was letting her die when something out there would cure her. I think this is a fairly natural and usual phase to go through for anyone in this situation as we cannot bear the thought of being so powerless. I think the 'language' of cancer, of 'fighting it', 'beating it', etc., does not help us when we have to accept that there is, in fact, nothing we can do. I pursued this for a while and then decided that I was chasing shadows.

In late 2014, the contract for the National Lung Cancer Audit (NLCA) was awarded to the Royal College of Physicians by the Healthcare Quality Improvement Partnership (HQIP) for three to five years. The contract did not include an audit for mesothelioma, and this audit is now independently funded by Mesothelioma UK.[25] This report makes several recommendations about how mesothelioma should be assessed and treated. Its main aim is to improve awareness of mesothelioma and set standards of how it should be treated. The audit itself is very interesting and I recommend that those with particular interest read it. It now certainly confirms for me that Rose received the most appropriate treatment and that her survival was no shorter than was to be expected.

---

[25] Royal College of Physicians. National Mesothelioma Audit report 2018 (for the audit period 2014–16). London: Royal College of Physicians, 2018

CHAPTER 6
Do Not Resuscitate

Whilst Rose was in the hospice a doctor came to discuss the DNAR (do not attempt resuscitation) form. I found this emotionally very difficult. I don't think that Rose quite twigged what the doctor was saying so I paraphrased for her. I can't remember what the doctor said, but I reflected on what I had said to people in similar situations – even to my own parents who had died three years previously. But on the whole, they had all been older people and somehow it felt very different having this conversation with a 33-year-old. I'm not sure I should have intervened in this process, but maybe I did it to help out the doctor who struggled to find the right words, or maybe I did it so that my confused daughter had no doubt what we were saying. She was not stupid and of course probably knew that no one would resuscitate her, but I don't think people think like that, even those who are terminally ill. I remember, as a GP trainee and then a GP trainer, learning, discussing and teaching how to break bad news, but I do not remember ever having discussed, role-played or taught ways to discuss the DNAR form. Perhaps that has changed in the few years since I was a trainer.

Rose took all this on board – the stopping of the chemotherapy, the DNAR form. She knew the score but didn't want to discuss it or have it spelt out for her. That's why the palliative care consultant was in such contrast to the oncology consultant. Having said that, the oncologist had the harder job, seeing Rose just after diagnosis.

As I watched her starving to death, I realised I wasn't ready for her to die. That may sound strange as, of course, I would never be 'ready' for this. I felt that she wasn't ready either, even though she was starving to death. However, I did tell my brother in the USA that I thought she wouldn't make Christmas and he came over. So did his daughter, all the way from San Francisco. More of that later. Luckily, we were rescued from this state of affairs by the palliative care consultant who went back to look over all her results and scans and notes and approached the problem from a fresh angle. He came up with a drug which is not an anti-sickness drug but which can be helpful in people with tumours of the small bowel (which Rose didn't have) and for other conditions. The drug is called octreotide. It was not one that I would ever have considered, but then I am not an expert in palliative care. I was, and am, truly grateful for this as it gave back her quality of life for a few months. The downside was that it had to go into a different syringe driver as it did not mix with what she was already having. So, Rose had two lines in her and two heavy drivers to carry around. The vomiting slowed down and she began to eat again. She also managed to get out to church and went to the carol service with her friends surrounding her. I have a lovely photo of this, with her in her new Christmas jumper that they bought for her.

Rose said she wanted to go home for Christmas, back to Cambridge. Everything was arranged with the district nurses and my surgery had to be involved to write up the drugs, etc. It was quite a feat of organisation but we managed it. Rose was very weak. An enduring memory is of her brother gently carrying her upstairs to bed and down again in the morning. I slept in the bed with her as I wouldn't have heard her call from my room. She really came alive in Cambridge and she made it to the King's College Christmas Day service with Bob and some friends. She also insisted on playing our annual traditional game of Settlers which she always won, but this time I pipped her to the post much to her disgust. David commented that he didn't think he would be so pleased to see her back to her bossy self. She saw friends from school and we had the biggest Christmas tree ever, thanks to our friend who had gone and bought it for us. She ate and enjoyed her Christmas dinner even though she vomited it back up again a few hours later. But the vomiting was down to about once a day and she was eating.

There was a blip when the GP wrote the wrong dose of one of the drugs on the prescription so on New Year's Day I had to try and negotiate the 111 and out-of-hours system again. Luckily, I spoke to a doctor I knew who did the script for me but none of the pharmacies that were open had it in stock so she had to do without it for 24 hours. I know the GP who had originally written the prescription was probably rushed and stressed in this pre-Christmas rush of demands on their time, but I was very frustrated as the prescription they wrote was illogical, in terms of the dose, and rather careless. It cost me a lot of hassle and Rose a lot of anxiety.

Predictably, when she got back to Oxford she stayed in bed and was very low. I think she felt that she would never go home again and certainly knew that it had been her last Christmas. She was so weak that I had to take her to the toilet and she had a couple of small fits followed by a fall which I couldn't prevent. I wondered about her haemoglobin, as did she, so I organised a blood test. Her haemoglobin was so low, at 34, it was barely compatible with life and none of the doctors had ever seen one so low. She needed another blood transfusion. The hospice was unfortunately full so she reluctantly went to the oncology triage ward. They were brilliant, gave her a side room and arranged a side room for me on the oncology ward for the night. She looked so ill that I thought she was going to die and I think the doctors and nurses thought the same. I wondered what would have happened if I hadn't been a doctor and not thought about the possible cause of these fits and collapse. Would it have been put down as part of the disease? Without that blood transfusion she surely would have died within a few days. I am sure that if I hadn't been there, she would have had more input from her GP who would have ordered a blood test. Sometimes I felt that the GPs were leaving it to me to alert them to things, recognise a problem, but that really wasn't my job. Having said that, I know that I behaved in such a way that I wanted to keep control so I don't blame them for leaving it to me. Again, the conflict of roles.

Rose weighed 48 kilogrammes when she went in for the transfusion. She had been a healthy 78 kilos, appropriate for her height of 5 foot 10 inches. She had lost a staggering 30 kilogrammes. As her kidney function had deteriorated, they wanted to do an ultrasound scan to see if the tumour was blocking her kidneys. I felt anxious and conflicted about the appropriateness of this as, even if that was a problem, it was unlikely she would survive any form of intervention. One becomes caught in this spiral of events, as with the district nurse doing the observations I described earlier when I was trying to get Rose into the hospice. If a problem is detected it is very hard not to go on to the next step, then the next, whether appropriate for the patient or not. This is best illustrated when doing a blood test to check if the prostate is healthy (a PSA test). Once an abnormal result is seen, then one has to go on to decide whether to do a biopsy, and if this shows any cancerous cells, the 'patient' has to decide whether to go on to treat it and what treatment to have. These cancerous cells may never go on to full blown cancer: there is a saying in the medical world that most men die with prostate cancer rather than because of it. But once on this treadmill it is hard to get off and a lot of anxiety can be caused for no good reason. Of course, there are cases where the cancer found at biopsy will go on to metastasise (spread) so treatment is appropriate. These difficult issues of investigating and finding abnormalities that may never cause a problem is becoming more common as people are demanding more screening. Luckily, in Rose's case, the ultrasound did not show any infiltration of the cancer to block the kidneys. Her kidneys were failing, but probably due to dehydration and the effects of medication. They could recover to some extent once she was able to drink more again.

CHAPTER 7
More positive times

We left the ward the next day. Rose's energy levels improved and she started eating again. The next step was to try and get rid of the syringe drivers, or at least one of them, as Rose hated carting them around. The palliative care nurse discussed it with the pharmacist at the hospice and she advised that there was an injection of a form of the octreotide that lasted for 28 days at a time. Rose agreed to try this and the vomiting slowed and then finally stopped. Whether this was the drug or the fact that the chemotherapy was finally out of her system, we don't know. Personally, I believed that the vomiting that continued long after the chemo had stopped indicated that the vomiting was more due to the disease than the chemo. Rose, however, did not like this theory because of its implication that the disease was causing this and therefore she would never be free of the syringe drivers or the distressing vomiting, so we didn't discuss it. Anyway, having vomited between 1 and 10 times a day for four months, it was a huge relief to her and to us who hated to see her so distressed. Her haemoglobin stabilised at a low level, suggesting that her bone marrow had started to recover after being hit by the chemotherapy. Although she had had only two rounds of chemotherapy it had nearly killed her and had made her life miserable. She would not contemplate going back to it. We will never know whether those two cycles extended her life or not, or whether more would have extended it further. She went back to see the respiratory consultant and this time I did not go into the consultation with her. I felt I needed to step back and let her express herself without me there. Also, there was no more information that I felt I needed at this point. She relayed to me that he had asked her whether she wanted to go back on the chemotherapy and she had told him that her quality of life was very important to her and that she didn't want to risk it. She told me that he agreed with her decision. She also agreed with her oncology nurse, who was in the consultation, that she would go back and see the oncology consultant.

I began to worry that I may be leading her into being too passive. Now she was feeling better, should we be thinking about having another virtual review by the Basingstoke doctors with another CT scan? We are surrounded by stories of people 'beating' cancer, or 'losing their fight' against cancer. I always think that it must make people feel guilty if they hadn't managed to 'beat it'. I don't like these messages because people are dying all the time from cancer that just isn't curable. I have always, as a doctor, found it hard to tread the line between giving false hope to my patients and giving them no hope at all. I had always been more towards the not giving false hope side, but maybe I was wrong. A friend brought this up in our conversation, saying I would probably find what she said annoying. Her husband, our friend, had died of a brain tumour 10 years previously and her thoughts about what people had said to her and their reactions I found useful. I wasn't annoyed with her suggestions, it just made me feel more tormented about what the right thing to do as a parent was. Now that Rose was feeling better, I felt in limbo … I knew that she wasn't going to survive this cancer but it seemed like the course of her illness was more difficult to predict. I had thought she would die of starvation and after that was partially solved, then bone marrow failure, but now she had overcome those threats, at least temporarily, it was hard to see what the final course of her illness would be. I thought I ought to get a 'second opinion' but after initiating the process by getting in touch with colleagues at Addenbrooke's Hospital in Cambridge, I realised that I was just falling prey to the 'positive thinking' line and that Rose was in one of the best hospitals in the country with access to experts in the field. I'm glad I didn't go further down that route, and Rose never asked me to. I never discussed my thoughts about this with her, so did not open the possibility of letting her choose. As a mother, I must try to pursue every angle, as relatives so often do, but as a doctor, I knew in my heart that this was offering a false hope. We are taught to reach decisions about treatment along with our patients. Is it really possible to do this when their knowledge is never going to be as complete as ours whatever we tell them or they read on the internet? Have we a duty to discourage them from spending money and precious time on treatments which have no scientific evidence to support them and which we know will not help them? Do we have the right to deny them hope? As I have said earlier, we usually have to tailor what we say to the person in front of us and the better we know them as GPs the better we can do this.

The months of February and March were a window when Rose was feeling better and was eating, though not putting on weight or getting stronger. She had periods when she vomited and always got demoralised then as she saw it as a retrograde step. Two trips she wanted to go on, and which I thought were pure fantasy, were to go to a spa and to go to the Harry Potter plays she had booked a year before.

After a lot of preparation (she had to be without the syringe driver for the day so we had to give an injection to try and tide her over) I drove to Woburn Centre Parcs with her. They were set up with wheelchairs and disabled access. To my amazement she walked around the spa all day. We had a great time. The only moment of sadness was when she was in their heated outdoor pool and she discovered that she couldn't swim because she couldn't float. So sad for someone who had always been such a great swimmer, and although she played it down, I knew that she was devastated by this, thinking of all the great times we had had as a family in holidays that revolved around swimming.

When she announced she wanted to go to London to see the two-part Harry Potter play she had booked, again I thought it a fantasy. But I realised how important it was for her to go, especially as she was going with her great childhood friend from Cambridge. When David and Harriet came down for the weekend, we talked about it and the possibility of getting a taxi. David immediately said he would go with her and Harriet jumped in eagerly to say they would love a day in London. So, on the day, they came down early to Oxford and went in a taxi together. They organised new seats in the theatre as Rose couldn't climb the steps. They even met her after the first play to wheel her to a restaurant with her friend and then pick her up again to take her back to the theatre. She loved it, stayed awake all day and evening and didn't vomit.

The next thing on her wish list was to go to our flat on Lake Como, where the whole story had started. Having learnt my lesson that these things were really important to her, and that they were achievable, we agreed we would go in June when the weather would be warm and sunny. But in reality, I knew that she would never get there and I think so did she.

Apart from these outings, during this time of relative recovery she was getting quite low in mood. She was bored and frustrated at her limitations, now really being confined to the wheelchair. She also wasn't sleeping well and, in a way, this was a harder time because she realised, I think, that she would never be able to do the things she loved to do again. She found it hard physically but also mentally. She hadn't been able to read to herself for a few months so I read to her every night. I read through a couple of Harry Potter books (the first time I had read them!) and other classics. I think she found it very upsetting that she couldn't read as this was such a joy to her. The other thing that made her sad was that she could not play the lovely new piano we had bought her the year before for her birthday. She just didn't have enough strength. I still find it amazing when I think about how much of what she had loved to do had become impossible and yet she very rarely moaned about it. Of course, you could say, as the reader, that she did not feel able to moan to me, that she couldn't open herself up to me as her mother. I agree, to some extent, but I don't think I am mistaken about Rose's basic personality – of stoicism and privacy. She did not moan to her close friends either, although I know that she had some opportunity to talk with them at a deeper level than with me. But she and I usually managed to communicate well, either positively or negatively, and I don't think she was particularly taciturn with me only.

Having said that, she was quite depressed: we did talk about that, and she said, "Of course I am!" With depression, the inability to sleep takes on a whole new dimension and is very distressing for people. An element of depression is due to chemical imbalance; I think that is generally accepted now. I'm sure this applied to her, given her inability to absorb any nutrients through her damaged stomach and bowel. The evidence for the most successful approach to depression is that a combination of medication and therapy is best. It was hard to enrol Rose in any formal therapy: she was offered music therapy at the hospice which she didn't really take to, and I luckily found a wonderful massage therapist for her which she really loved. Other than that, she was quite resistant to that approach, as many depressed people are, as she didn't see how it was going to help her. She had so many reasons to be depressed, being someone who was grieving for their own life. I thought some mirtazapine (a sedating antidepressant which would hopefully at least help her sleep) might help and after discussing it with the consultant, she started it.

I also found this period hard. She was stable and it was easy to forget that she was dying. I occasionally remembered with a jolt and I was fearful for her about how her death would be. When she was not eating and was so weak, I thought she would just fade away. Now I thought of all the horrible things that could happen with this tumour, like bowel obstruction or a massive internal bleed.

We went back to see the oncology consultant and the meeting seemed more relaxed, more friendly. She was gentle with Rose and I thought I saw tears in her eyes. A couple of days later I bumped into her with her daughter in the street. Her daughter was 10 or 11 and I know that tears were there, because however resilient we are as doctors, when faced with pain and sadness, we cannot, as mothers, bear to see a mother who will be mourning the loss of their child. Of course, that is a projection from what I have always felt, but I know other doctors who feel the same.

I didn't know it, but this was the end of the 'good period'.

CHAPTER 8
What is empathy?

I have alluded to the differences in how clinicians communicate with patients and which seemed more appropriate to Rose.

It could be said that 'empathy' is a key concept here. That clinicians who lack empathy cannot communicate as well with patients. The concept is quite philosophically difficult, and I will come to that. I was struck, when listening to Henry Marsh on Desert Island Discs recently, by how he defended the assertion that all surgeons are cool and unable to show empathy to their patients. He said, in loose terms, that it may be that surgeons, who delve around in our bodies and for whom the slightest mistake may have devastating consequences, in some sense need to maintain a distance from the patient for their own survival.

Rather than emotional disengagement, Decety believes that:

> doctors must learn to accept their own empathic feelings toward patients, yet not confuse their feelings with those of their patients, so that they can respond in the best way possible. This important discernment can become difficult when physicians are working under stressful conditions. In other words, stress—not emotion—is the true enemy of the caring physician.[26]

But the whole idea of being empathic is not only to understand a patient's fears and feelings. It is important that we also understand how our patient wants us to respond and what they want us to do. Some doctors Rose met did not show that level of understanding and respect when telling her of her diagnosis or prognosis. So, the skill is not only to be able to be empathetic but also to know when and how it is appropriate to be so.

---

[26] Ezequiel Gleichgerrcht and Jean Decety The relationship between different facets of empathy, pain perception and compassion fatigue among physicians

Philosophically then, what is empathy and is it possible to achieve it?

Ramsey McNabb discusses this:

Tragically, Hector's father is involved in a car accident and dies. Hector is devastated. An acquaintance, Anita, tells him that she knows just how he feels. Angered at her presumption, he responds, "No, you don't know how I feel!" After all, how could she know how he feels? She doesn't know what he is going through, what he is thinking and how he is feeling. No one can know how anyone else feels.

But here lies the paradox. If he claims that she cannot know how he feels, he is necessarily making an assertion about how she feels! If it is true that one person cannot know how another person feels, then it follows that he cannot know how she feels, and hence, he cannot know that she doesn't know how he feels. His position is self-defeating. If he is right, he is wrong.[27]

The first statement is intuitively true – no one can ever know how another person feels or thinks. It follows deductively, therefore, that no one can know that others have not had identical feelings.

But in the world of medicine, this is a false dilemma. No doctor should ever say that they know how their patient feels. But can they even understand what the other person feels?

Mohammadreza Hojat, the director of Thomas Jefferson University's Longitudinal Study of Medical Education, believes that what medical students need is more training in "cognitive empathy" – an understanding of experiences, concerns, and perspectives of the patient and the ability to communicate that understanding. He distinguishes cognitive empathy (which he just calls 'empathy') from 'affective empathy', which he calls 'sympathy', or the emotional response that a physician might experience in response to a patient. Several of his studies

---

[27] Ramsey McNabb Philosophy Now Vol 52

have shown positive correlations between physicians' cognitive empathy and improved patient outcomes.[28]

So, what is the difference between empathy and sympathy?

David Jeffrey discusses the differences between empathy, sympathy and compassion.

Empathy is a complex, multifaceted, dynamic concept which has been described in the literature in many different ways. So, it appears that empathy means different things to different people. The conceptualisation of empathy has evolved in different ways relating to differing disciplines such as medicine, nursing, philosophy, psychology and counselling. This evolution can be best illustrated by addressing four dimensions of empathy: affective, cognitive, behavioural and moral. However, in practice, these four dimensions interact and overlap to differing extents in differing contexts in different clinical situations.

Sympathy takes a 'self-orientated' perspective which may arise from an egoistic motivation to help the other person in order to relieve one's own distress. In taking such a self-orientated perspective, the doctor risks being distressed or overwhelmed.

Compassion in its drive to alleviate suffering also shares elements of altruism. However, one can feel compassionate concern for another without making any attempt to understand their feelings and point of view.

In concluding his interesting discussion, he comes down heavily on the side of empathy, but empathy is something that must be acquired or taught.

---

[28] Jill Suttie Should we train doctors for empathy? Greater Good Magazine, July 2015

Empathy, unlike compassion or sympathy, is not something that just happens to us, it is a choice to make to pay attention to extend ourselves. It requires an effort.[29]

Daniel Sokol questions whether empathy can be taught and also challenges whether it is a desirable quality at all. He argues that doctors need to maintain a degree of dispassion. But is he here conflating empathy with sympathy?

A key problem with empathy is that it cannot readily be taught to those who are not, by nature, empathetic. You cannot teach empathy as you teach how to perform a lumbar puncture. In that respect, there is much to be said for focusing on less nebulous qualities, such as courtesy and politeness. As I have argued previously, these are undervalued traits in medicine, and although their importance may be obvious their application is more challenging in the heat of a busy clinic, when frustration and fatigue can test even the most patient doctor.

Aside from the difficulty in teaching empathy, it is debatable whether it is a desirable quality for doctors. Indeed, the ill effects of empathy underpin the reason why doctors should not treat loved ones. A degree of dispassion is needed to maintain a medical gaze not blurred by too great a concern for the patient as a person. Yet, the questionable benefits of empathy do not derogate from the importance of kindness, which is a less demanding emotion. Few patients would object to a kind doctor. Many more would have

---

[29] David Jeffrey: Empathy, sympathy and compassion in healthcare: Is there a problem? Is there a difference? Does it matter? Journal of the Royal Society of Medicine, December 6, 2016

concerns about an empathic doctor, fearing this shows either inexperience or a lack of mental fortitude[30]

In my experience as a GP, I have worked with others who become, in my view, too emotionally involved with their patients. This can lead to a dependent relationship which is not good for the doctor or the patient. The doctor can 'burn out' and the patient can become incapable of taking responsibility for their own health.

I agree to some extent with Daniel Sokol in that empathy is a characteristic that not every doctor naturally has, and I have seen many trainees who do not seem to grasp the concept. I once brought up in a clinical meeting the issue of patients who cry in the consultation, as I had just had a morning of tears and tissues. One of the GPs who had been practising for 30 years said that no patient ever cried in their consultations. Initially I was shocked at this, but they were a very popular doctor. I realised that patients choose who they see according to how they want to be dealt with and that some doctors just do not 'allow' patients that emotion and some patients do not want it. I can actually remember myself once, being in a fragile state, not wanting to see a particular doctor because I knew that her 'empathy' in the consultation would probably lead to me losing control of my emotions and I didn't want that.

I think the two things that are most important in a consultation are the ability of the doctor to leave enough silent spaces for the story to come out, and to be kind. A recent editorial in the British Medical Journal has elevated the status of kindness:

Kindness has for too long been described in apologetic terms and people are reluctant to use it as a tool because "it's seen as soft and fluffy."⁴ Perhaps we need to start valuing kindness for what it really is—the hard edged, mission focused, business end of healthcare.[31]

So how does this relate to Rose's story and all the different contacts she had with clinicians?

---

[30] Daniel Sokol BMJ June 2012

[31] R.E. Klaber. Kindness: an underrated currency. BMJ 20th December 2019. Editorial

I describe the different interactions throughout the book. I think there were only two doctors who really went anywhere near understanding Rose and how she wanted to be treated. The palliative care consultant reflected back to her what he thought she might be thinking/feeling but not in a way that demanded any reply. The respiratory consultant actually managed to get her to talk. The district nurses again were kind and got varying responses from her. I still am not sure that I understand exactly what it was that got through to her, and she was my daughter. Obviously, as I said above, it depends enormously on how much the patient wants to tell you. My conclusion? Be kind to your patients, however they respond to you.

CHAPTER 9
Friends and family

When it became clear how ill Rose was and that Bob and I would be in Oxford looking after her, the members of Rose's church in Headington organised a meal rota and church members unfailingly brought round lovely meals twice a week every week for months. Unfortunately, Rose could not always enjoy these meals. When she managed to get to church, she was surrounded by people offering their good wishes, love and prayers. This was not always welcome and tired her enormously, but she would rarely let them see this.

There was never any question about my staying in Oxford when we knew the diagnosis. We had always been close, despite some prickliness and impatience she showed to me on occasions (and vice versa). She was a very private person and I learnt not to ask her direct questions about her life, knowing that eventually she would tell me something and then I would have an opening to talk about it. This tactic had to be used with her illness. I knew she understood the significance of the diagnosis but she didn't want to be made to think about it except when she felt able to. In her own time, she would say something that gave me an opening and then I could explore it in more depth. I learnt not to interfere in her dealings with doctors and nurses, though this was sometimes very hard and I couldn't help myself. I think many of the clinicians thought that we did not get on well, did not communicate with each other. On one occasion when I was not there, Rose told me that her oncology nurse had commented that it seemed like she didn't get on with her mum. Rose was angry about this and told me about it indignantly afterwards. I also was irritated: she hardly knew us and had jumped to this conclusion after a difficult consultation where Rose had been told her prognosis. It made me reflect on how I often jumped to conclusions about my patient's relationships and how I often failed to explore the context. It must be said that this oncology specialist nurse was very kind, calm and helpful and a fantastic support as time went on, and I held no grudges about a throw-away comment she made probably because she was finding it hard to communicate with Rose. Similarly, with the oncology consultant. These women had their own children and no doubt they found it emotionally hard to have such a young patient. Rose certainly did not make it easy for many of the clinicians with whom she came in contact.

During these difficult months, David and Harriet were fantastic. They came every weekend from Coventry and when Rose was very ill, before Christmas, they stayed for two weeks. They also stayed for two weeks in May when it was obvious that Rose was not going to live much longer. They always put her first, despite having stressful work lives themselves. Rose really appreciated it and was generous in her thanks. It made me very proud of my son and very grateful that he had chosen such a wonderful wife. Rose and David had had a difficult relationship as children, but it had been improving and for several years they had been much closer. One of the first things she said when she was diagnosed was that they must try and work out where she had been exposed to asbestos as he might have been exposed too. In the same vein, she would get very upset in the beginning, asking who would look after me when I was old (Bob is a lot older than me and she assumed I would be left on my own by his death). I was amazed that she could think of others when she had her own life to grieve.

Bob found it very difficult to be with Rose at the beginning. He would cry and not know what to say to her. I tried to tell him that he must not cry in front of her as it made her very upset, and that he should just behave normally on a day-to-day basis. I was privileged as I had to do a lot of personal care and found it easier to be with her so she would come out with bits of information about how she was feeling, her fears and concerns. I just had to wait for it to come from her in her own time. I think this is a skill I learnt as a GP, to let people tell their stories and not to fire questions at them; to give them time.

My brother and new sister-in-law, Tony and Mary, who live in Sussex, came up several times, bearing gifts and food. Rose had recently been to their wedding in Spain with me and we were very fond of Mary who was great for Tony. They were so thoughtful and supportive during this time. Tony's first wife, who had known Rose well as she grew up, was also very thoughtful and sent cards and messages. My brother, who lives in America, made a trip over to visit us when we thought she might not survive until Christmas, and his daughter, a very busy woman, made a special trip from San Francisco for a few days just to see her. Another of my nieces visited a few times from London and even brought her mother. She had been divorced for over 30 years from my eldest brother, who had recently died. My family were tremendous.

My friends came regularly from Cambridge, and a friend from France came. Even friends from Australia managed to manufacture an extended business trip and came down to see us. I had two great friends in Oxford and they were always ready to listen to me or see me as I needed. It was all a great help to me and I think it helped Rose too to see that I had support.

Rose's friends and colleagues were astonishingly consistent and sustained in the way they were there for her. Someone came practically every day. Church friends came around often and it touched me greatly that they continued with the meal rota for the nine months of her illness. Her two closest church friends and I kept up to date via WhatsApp. Sometimes, when Rose felt more nauseous than usual or didn't have the energy to talk, she would pretend to be asleep, but they understood this and were patient with her. One of her friends, George, even managed to talk to Rose about her funeral and what songs and readings she would like. This was something I just couldn't do and am forever grateful to her for that.

Her colleagues, also friends, were mainly doctors who had worked with Rose on their various research projects in the Neurosciences Unit at the John Radcliffe. They came when she wanted them and left her alone when she didn't. They took her out in the wheelchair for 'lunch' and were always very lively. They organised a book of photos and comments from her colleagues and brought good wishes and presents. They organised Harry Potter events and meals at the flat.

Her friends from her Cambridge childhood found it difficult being so far away, but they came to see her from Cambridge, Sussex and Stoke. They brought their children, presents and news, and again, a book of photographs of the lives they had shared with Rose growing up together. I think they found it hard because they weren't around to live through her illness with her like her Oxford friends. These friends who had known her the longest – Emily had been friends with Rose since she was four years old – I'm sure were very sad that they could not be with her very often.

There were other random friends from all parts of Rose's life. It is not easy to maintain this kind of support and kindness over many months of illness, and it comforted me to see how loved Rose was, but also made me sad to see what she would be leaving behind.

One of the most difficult things to deal with as Rose got sicker and weaker was trying to control the number of people who came to see her. I became the 'gatekeeper'. I would sometimes ask her and she might reply that she didn't want to see them and we all had to respect that. I tried to give priority to her closest friends but it became very difficult. I understood that they wanted to spend time with her and say goodbye to her. They had needs too and I didn't want to deny them this important time but Rose found it very tiring and would often close her eyes and pretend to be asleep as she didn't have the energy to engage with them. I didn't enjoy being the 'gatekeeper' but I think it was important to her. Her friends said she didn't answer their texts and emails, and I had to try to soften the hurt that they felt. One good friend, Tim, had been with Rose on the church camps and in the group she was in at church. He had been ordained during their friendship at another local church, and he would just sit with her for hours and hold her hand or read prayers quietly. He was gentle and kind and I had no qualms about calling him and asking him to sit with Rose and give her spiritual support. The other thing she never refused was a massage from my Oxford friend, Netia, , who struck just the right note with Rose. Rose really looked forward to her massage even to the end. It helped me too as I felt that it was something very positive that I could organise for her.

CHAPTER 10
The end of the reprieve

In April the nausea and vomiting returned, with the added challenge of insomnia. I would lie with her a as I knew how lonely and frightening it must have been to lie awake at night. Rose was usually so strong and so stoical but one morning, whilst I was doing some work on my computer, I heard a strange noise from her room and I rushed in to find that she was sobbing. All she could say was that she wanted her life back, and the pain of loss shot through me as I realised, again, that this period of looking after a 'sick child' would not last forever and that I would lose her. I could only hold her close – how could I comfort this anguish she felt?

We went back to see the palliative care consultant and he went through how the drugs might be affecting her and what else they could try. He gave her plenty of opportunity to talk about her feelings, fears and thoughts but also told her that some people didn't want to talk and that that was OK. That evening we talked about depression and she said that of course she was 'depressed', because who wouldn't be? That was how it was and she didn't think antidepressants would help her. I realised that she was right, that she had her way of dealing with things and it didn't involve talking to people or taking drugs that had no meaning for her. It may not be how I would have dealt with the situation, but how would I ever know that? However, I had to respect her way of dealing with it. I must give her the opportunity to make her own decisions, in the same way that I tried to with my patients. As doctors, even now trained as they are in communication skills, 'shared decision making' and other buzz phrases, we think we know the best thing for our patients. Often we do, but sometimes we do not really listen to what they are saying, or not saying. It is so difficult to tread that line, and I realised that yes, I am good at listening to patients, but that I don't always accept that they don't want to talk to me. The kind of relationship that allows us to really act in our patient's best interests is built up over months and years. What is going to happen to this relationship now that general practice is moving towards the model of 'walk-in' clinics', 'same day appointments' with any doctor who is available? The continuity that is crucial to good communication is getting lost, and that is very sad.

Meanwhile, Rose was almost constantly nauseous now and she vomited about once a day. There was also a new symptom of pain in her back and sides and in her shoulder. These pains were not constant but could be quite severe. I asked the GP to write up some stat doses (given when necessary) of morphine, and this could be given through her line. The vomiting changed: now she was also vomiting at night and it was copious amounts of greeny black fluid. She woke often, thinking she was going to vomit, but then was not able to. She was very downhearted and asked me why, in this country, people couldn't decide they had 'had enough'. She said she would rather die now as she was going to anyway and she was so fed up with the nausea and vomiting. She wouldn't go out, except to the Hospice Day Centre which she enjoyed. During one of these visits, she saw the palliative care consultants who persuaded her to stay in to try and get on top of the vomiting again. She was very reluctant but agreed. She spent four nights there and came out with one of the dreaded syringe drivers back. She also had another blood transfusion but these transfusions only really kept her haemoglobin up for a couple of weeks.

The vomiting did improve, though, and she went home. She had a terrible night when the diarrhoea was pouring out of her and she was so weak it was very hard to get her to the bathroom and to clean her up. She fell to the floor at one point and I managed to get her back up again – she may not have weighed much but she was very tall and difficult to pick up. I called Hospital at Home who very kindly brought loperamide (an anti-diarrhoea drug) out to her at 4 a.m. She stayed in bed all the time now, except for one mammoth effort when David and Harriet were there and she wanted to take them out for lunch as it was a beautiful May day. We managed to get her in the car and drove out to the country and sat in a pub garden. I could see she was suffering sitting waiting for lunch. She had ordered a meal but only ate two chips. We wanted to wheel her along the canal but it was too hot and the bumpy path gave her pain. After this, she didn't go out again, not even to the day centre.

David came and stayed, forgoing a wedding he was supposed to go to where Harriet was maid of honour. He carried Rose from bed to couch and helped her sit up in bed in her quest to be more comfortable. I could just about manage to get her onto the commode. The wonderful district nurses built more time into their visits so they could help me wash her. Nights were very disturbed because she couldn't sit up on her own and if she felt sick, I had to try and sit her up, and then she wasn't sick. She also liked me to lie with her when she couldn't sleep. The nurses and GP kept asking me if I wanted carers or a Marie Curie nurse to help. I felt I wanted to do it all myself as she did not have long left and then I could sleep as much as I wanted. Why wouldn't I want to give her all the time and care I could? I did agree to try a Marie Curie nurse one night to see how it went. I slept through till 5 a.m. when she woke me to give Rose her drugs as she was in pain. She couldn't do this as she was not a nurse. Poor Rose told me I was getting grumpy because I was so tired and I should 'go away' for a rest. It broke my heart – how could I possibly leave her even to go to the shops now? I promised I would try very hard not to be grumpy! Again, the conflict of roles – she wanted a mum, but she didn't want a stranger to care for her so I had to be both, and also at some points a doctor too.

My brother and sister-in-law came to visit from the States; it was a planned visit to the UK. Also, my nieces from the States were in England. My poor sister-in-law was so shocked by the sight of Rose who she had not seen in the early days of the illness. My nieces were also very saddened to see her. She couldn't really talk to them but I think she really appreciated them coming and told me she felt guilty she couldn't 'entertain' them.

Into May and her decline was quite obvious. I started sleeping with her, as she called me so often in the night it was just easier to do so. It also felt like the natural thing to do. One night she needed to pee and I managed to get her onto the commode but then she fainted. It was a real struggle to get her back into bed. I decided it was no longer safe to try and get her sitting or standing on my own. Luckily, Rose has always had a strong bladder, able to go 12 hours without peeing. We got a bed pan and used pads.

Days and nights became the same – she would sleep and call out all day and all night. She ate nothing. David carried her into the living room so we could all watch *Lord of the Rings*. It was one of her favourite films and was so familiar to her that it didn't matter if she slept through bits. Halfway through the third film of the trilogy, I realised she would not get to the end because it was just too uncomfortable for her to lie on the settee. One thing we did together after she died was watch the rest of the film together.

One night she was sick, she was itching, she was in pain from her minor bed sores and I said, as you do, "Oh, Rose, what are we going to do with you?' Her instant reply was, "Put me down."

Yet she rarely got distressed, seemed quite calm except when her pressure points were troubling her. The amount of morphine I was giving her increased slowly but was still a miniscule amount for palliative care. She steadfastly refused to have a second syringe driver through which she could have a steady dose of morphine.

April and early May were very hard for me. Spring had arrived and new life was everywhere. Rose couldn't get out much to see it and when I did, it made me incredibly sad to see such a stark contrast of the new life surrounding me whilst hers was ebbing away in such a distressing fashion.

CHAPTER 11

Assisted Dying

Rose's comment about wishing people in this country could choose when they died prompted me to think again about the assisted dying debate.

In the last four years there have been four attempts to pass a bill on assisted dying through parliament.

The first was Lord Falconer's Bill in 2014, then Rob Maris' Bill in 2015, Lord Hayward's Bill in 2016 and finally, but only applying to Guernsey, the Bill in 2018. None of these bills have been passed into law.

The argument has been helpfully summed up as follows:

Arguments for

- Freedom of choice: advocates argue that the patient should be able to make their own choice.
- Quality of life: Only the patient really knows how they feel, and how the physical and emotional pain of illness and prolonged death impacts their quality of life.
- Dignity: Every individual should be able to die with dignity.
- Witnesses: Many who witness the slow death of others believe that assisted death should be allowed.
- Resources: It makes more sense to channel the resources of highly-skilled staff, equipment, hospital beds, and medications towards life-saving treatments for those who wish to live, rather than those who do not.
- Humane: It is more humane to allow a person with intractable suffering to be allowed to choose to end that suffering.
- Loved ones: It can help to shorten the grief and suffering of loved ones.

- We already do it: If a beloved pet has intractable suffering, it is seen as an act of kindness to put it to sleep. Why should this kindness be denied to humans?

Arguments against

- The doctor's role: Health care professionals may be unwilling to compromise their professional roles, especially in the light of the Hippocratic Oath. ("I will neither give a deadly drug to anybody who asked for it, nor will I make a suggestion to this effect.")
- Moral and religious arguments: Several faiths see euthanasia as a form of murder and morally unacceptable. Suicide, too, is 'illegal' in some religions. Morally, there is an argument that euthanasia will weaken society's respect for the sanctity of life.
- Patient competence: Euthanasia is only voluntary if the patient is mentally competent, with a lucid understanding of available options and consequences, and the ability to express that understanding and their wish to terminate their own life. Determining or defining competence is not straightforward.
- Guilt: Patients may feel they are a burden on resources and are psychologically pressured into consenting. They may feel that the financial, emotional, and mental burden on their family is too great. Even if the costs of treatment are provided by the state, there is a risk that hospital personnel may have an economic incentive to encourage euthanasia consent.
- Mental illness: A person with depression is more likely to ask for assisted suicide, and this can complicate the decision.
- Slippery slope: There is a risk that physician-assisted suicide will start with those who are terminally ill and wish to die because of intractable suffering, but then begin to include other individuals.

- Possible recovery: Very occasionally, a patient recovers, against all the odds. The diagnosis might be wrong.
- Palliative care: Good palliative care makes euthanasia unnecessary.
- Regulation: Euthanasia cannot be properly regulated.[32]

In a recent BMJ, a head-to-head debate covered some of these points: Terry English argues that there were plenty of safeguards in the Falconer Bill, including the competency of the patient who requests assisted suicide and who has a terminal condition with less than six months to live. He argues that in Oregon there is a superb palliative care system and that they have not seen evidence of the 'slippery slope'. Individual cases have been decided in the Courts in England and the rulings usually echo Lord Donaldson in 2002 who stated that the right of the individual is paramount.

Arguing against the establishment of a law, Bernard Ribeiro argues that the law must protect the more vulnerable who may feel that the doctor they trust thinks they should ask for assisted suicide and there may be undue pressure on the patient/doctor relationship.[33]

Whatever the moral arguments, there have been several surveys to discover the beliefs of the general public and of doctors. The British Social Attitudes Survey:

> In contrast with UK law, there is strong support (78%) for allowing voluntary euthanasia where it is carried out by a doctor for a person with an incurable disease. The overall trend has been relatively stable over time. It appeared as if there was a slow trend towards increasing support between 1983 and 1994, but that has now halted and the levels of support for voluntary euthanasia are the same in 2016 as in 1983.
> Those with no religion being most likely to support euthanasia (for example, 89% of people without a

---

[32] https://www.medicalnewstoday.com

[33] BMJ 7 Feb. 2018 P360: https://doi.org/10.1136/bmj.k562

religion say euthanasia by a doctor for someone with a terminal disease should be allowed, compared with 67% of people with a religion).

In general, there are also some differences by age; those in the oldest age groups (75+) tend to be less supportive of euthanasia than younger age groups. For example, 77% of the youngest age group say euthanasia by a doctor for someone who will die from a painful disease should be allowed, compared with 69% of the oldest age group. However, it is the middle age groups who are most likely to approve of voluntary euthanasia in this situation, with 85% of 45-54 year olds and 84% of 55-64 year olds saying this'[34]

But what about doctors? The major organisations for doctors are opposed to assisted dying:

The BMA and the key medical royal colleges remain opposed to assisted dying. So too do the American Medical Association, the American College of Physicians, and the American Academy of Family Physicians, despite assisted dying being legally available to 58 million Americans in six states and the District of Columbia. These organisations' positions have long been out of step with the general public: polls in the UK and the US have suggested more than 80% support for assisted dying. More worryingly, their positions seem also now to be out of step with doctors.[35]

However, the Royal College of Physicians have recently declared that they are neutral on the question of assisted dying. This was based on a survey of its members where three questions were asked. There was a majority in favour of not changing the law (43.4%) but a total majority

---

[34] http://www.bsa.natcen.ac.uk/media/39147/bsa34_moral_issues_final.pdf

[35] BMJ Ibid

of those wanting it changed (31.6%) plus those wanting the College to be neutral (25%). [36]

This has caused an outburst of discussion amongst doctors, many very critical of the Royal College for taking this 'neutral' stance. Meanwhile, a recent poll of the members of the Royal College of General Practitioners, nearly 50,000 GPs, showed that 47% were against a change in the law, 40% supported a change in the law and 11% supported a neutral stance. The RCGP subsequently stated that the College would continue to oppose a change. This report came out on 21st February 2020. It could be argued that this was against the wishes of members as 51% supported a change or a neutral stance: it could have taken the same position as the RCP.

The major medical bodies (apart from the RCP) and parliament seem to be out of step with the majority opinion. There are good arguments for further debate and for careful consideration of the safeguards put in place. Sabine Netters, a doctor in Holland, outlines the Dutch Law:

Euthanasia is punishable under Dutch law unless six conditions are met: the patient's request is voluntary and persists over time; the patient's suffering is unbearable with no prospect of improvement; the patient is fully aware of his situation; and there is no alternative. These conditions must be verified by an independent doctor. And the process must be carried out with due medical care (a protocol stipulates the exact dose of sedative and barbiturate).

It seems that a very powerful lobby against assisted dying comes from those clinicians working in palliative care. The argument is that if palliative care is of the highest standard then there is no place for assisted suicide. They do recognise, however, that patients' experiences of palliative care vary across the country. Rose was in Oxford and her palliative care was exemplary. Although she was not in pain, her symptoms were such that her life was made miserable and these were not ever fully controlled. Her mental anguish was also hard to bear and hard to watch despite her strong Christian belief. I don't think palliative care

---

[36] https://www.rcplondon.ac.uk/news/no-majority-view-assisted-dying-moves-rcp-position-neutral

can ever really help someone, especially a young person, grieve the life they are going to lose. Although she can be said to have had a 'good death', the last few days and weeks were very distressing to her and to her family and friends and there seemed no point in delaying her death. Luckily, her family were with her when she died, but we may not have been and it must be very distressing for close relatives to be haunted with the thought that the person they loved so much died alone. A planned death would ensure that everyone who wanted to be there could be.

I think this is a topic that will continue to be discussed and the law to be challenged, and I think that sometime in the future the law will be changed.

Since writing this the Royal College of General Practitioners has taken a neutral stance on the question.

CHAPTER 12

The last days

I now thought that her friends should come and see her if they wanted, but only to sit and talk to her, hold her hand, say a prayer, and not more than two at a time. I don't know what she felt about this but I thought that it was important to her friends to say goodbye. I'm sure they found it very distressing to see this skeletal shadow who was once their lively, funny, caring friend. It was getting harder to keep a grip on my emotions but I just had to keep going. We all took it in turns to sit with her, mainly so she knew we were with her, but also because I did not want her to be alone when she took her last breath.

I slept in her bed with her on the Friday and Saturday nights, as I had been doing most of the time in the last week or so. On Friday night she wanted the commode. I struggled to get her on and she fainted and I could only just hold her and pull her back to bed. I realised it was no longer safe for her to get out of bed. On Saturday night she kept saying she couldn't breathe and I was struggling to sit her up but then she had some pain and I had to lie her down again. She seemed quite anxious and I gave her a small dose of morphine and some midazolam (a strong sedative). On Sunday morning she seemed calm but her breathing had changed. I decided that the district nurse should put up the second syringe driver as Rose would not know and I didn't want her to be in pain. I sat with her most of the morning, and David and Harriet came in and out. Bob went to church. She was moaning a bit, though barely conscious and I gave her another small dose of morphine. Bob came back from church and a friend brought lunch round for us. I told Bob to go and sit with Rose. I knew from her breathing that the end was near, but when David came in as we were setting out lunch and asked me to go into her bedroom as he thought she had stopped breathing, it was still a shock to see her take her last breaths, as I have seen others do. She looked peaceful and we all kissed her goodbye. I felt bad for our friend as she had lost her husband, and our good friend, to cancer and it must have brought it all back. I texted Rose's closest friends to tell them and invited them to come and see her if they wanted to. I was in no rush to see her taken away but I sensed that David, at least, would rather she be collected sooner rather than later. So, after the out-of-hours paramedic had been to confirm death, I called the funeral directors. Having confirmed the death of so many people myself, usually during my out-of-hours shifts, it was strange to watch someone come and do so for my daughter. I felt caught again between being a mother and being a doctor. Four of Rose's friends came and I left them to say their goodbyes. Once the funeral directors had been and taken Rose, I was desperate to be on my own. Everyone left and I climbed into her bed and howled.

We had been the actors in a scene that is rarely played out these days. Most people with terminal illnesses die in hospital or a hospice. Rose died surrounded by her close family who loved her dearly. She did not utter any meaningful last words and we never had a conversation that is possible with older people, about how they had lived a good life and were grateful for that. Her body was now so emaciated that she was barely recognisable. We all had spent many hours sitting with her and had said our silent goodbyes and so I felt no regret that I wasn't there to hold her hand in her last moments. She had just slipped peacefully away and for that we must be forever grateful.

It brought back memories for me of my parents' deaths four years earlier. My father had had sepsis and was in hospital, hooked up to various machines to keep him alive. It was very sudden and unpredicted. I had a frank discussion with the consultant who said that he wouldn't recover. I called my siblings and asked the doctor to take my father off the machines and let him die peacefully. I have always regretted that I was not with him in the early hours when he died, that he died alone. I had my poor mother, who was in the early stages of dementia, to look after and a job to go to. I have managed to shed that guilt. My mother died about six weeks later after a fall. I tried very hard to keep her in her home, refusing to let the ambulance crew take her to hospital as I knew she didn't want that (though she agreed to their suggestion in a typically passive way!). I couldn't look after her despite living in her flat with her for a while, and so found a bed in a care home that I knew from visiting the residents many times as a GP. She was sad and was waiting to die to join her beloved husband of 70 years. After about the third day, I was there in the evening and then had to go to the football (I was the doctor for Cambridge United). I told her I would tell her the score the next morning. I got a phone call halfway through the match saying she had just collapsed and died, so I went there, abandoning my job to a friend who was with me who was also a doctor. She looked peaceful. I felt that this was the way she would have wanted to die and I felt I had said my goodbyes. My parents had had a wonderful life together and their deaths were peaceful and painless, and they believed they were going to a better life.

Rose also believed that, and her death was a 'good' death, but her suffering had been great. Not pain, not even the terrible vomiting and nausea, but the psychological pain of having lived a life so full, so nourished by her faith and her friends which was so difficult to leave. Her grieving for her life was unbearable, but she had been so strong and so dignified in her grief.

CHAPTER 13

Our journey together

Throughout this nine-month period, Rose and I lived together in the same small flat, with others coming and going but I never left her for more than a couple of hours that whole time. It is difficult to know what we did with all that time. We watched a lot of television, having our daily fix of *Neighbours*. We also went through box sets of more cerebral things like *Line of Duty* and *Call the Midwife*. A lot of the things we watched involved someone dying and people grieving, and I did wonder how she felt when this happened but she never gave any indication that she wanted to stop watching them. Perhaps she was able to separate the fiction from her own experience. She never said anything, so neither did I, but I often found it very hard to watch these painful scenes. We also watched an awful lot of *A Place in the Sun*! I think these mindless programmes are very addictive and we often went around each episode more than once. However, I think Rose ultimately got fed up with watching endless sun and sea and people's dreams and fantasies. There really is only so much *A Place in the Sun* a human brain can take!

At the beginning we went out a bit, often to lunch in a pub, or for a drive. We went to Waitrose together and, of course, we went to many appointments at the hospital. We went to the cinema a couple of times and to restaurants which was always nice. I think she enjoyed those trips but she was often quick to be sharp tongued, to me especially, and her mood was never that good. But then, how could it be? The fact that she didn't curl up in her bed and give up is a great credit to her. How can someone so young 'enjoy' things when she knows that it may be the last time she does it, that she won't be around to see the next summer, or Christmas? She got so bored too, having worked in a job as a medical statistician that required a good brain, solving people's problems, writing papers and going to meetings and conferences. Her world had shrunk and she had to take pleasure from things that she would never usually be bothered with. I never talked about these things with her, sensing that she just didn't want to. I hope I was right.

I don't really know now where the time went. It seemed that days were so long but that her time with me was so short. I think she was frightened that I would get fed up with looking after her, or too exhausted, and she used to tell me to take time off, to do things, even to go away. In a way she was right, but how could I go away when every moment was precious? I did go swimming throughout the winter in the heated outdoor pool at the gym. And I did go into town or out with my friends for lunch or coffee, but I could not go away.

As she got thinner and sicker, I often wondered what people thought; whether they thought she was anorexic, for example. That would be the main cause for someone her age being so thin and debilitated. Despite her difficulty with eating, she was keen to go out for nice meals and my friends, Netia and Wendy, did us proud when we went around to their houses. The last time she went to Wendy's, Wendy had made her favourite pasta dish and Rose ate so much of it that I was astounded. That was her last proper meal.

The days were mapped out by the daily visit of the district nurses to change her syringe driver, having lunch, watching some telly, having supper and then the trip to bed. She went through a phase when she didn't want to go to bed because she had fallen asleep on the sofa and didn't want to move. She would pretend to be asleep, or truly be really drowsy from the drugs, and I would desperately try to wake her and get her to bed because I felt I couldn't relax until she was settled, and I really needed to have a space on my own. It was a bit like having a stubborn child and it culminated in a row one evening when we both got upset. I ended up leaving her on the settee and she called me about midnight to go to bed. I realised that I was being unreasonable because it was up to her to decide when she went to bed. But I think she understood that it was a stress on me because she wanted, and later needed, me to help her get ready for bed. We made our peace; I tried very hard not to treat her as a child and she tried hard to wake herself up. I read to her every night because after the first few weeks of her illness she found it impossible to concentrate on reading, and later to physically hold the book. We got through quite a few books, and this was my introduction to Harry Potter as I read through the tomes. But we never finished the last book we started together, *I capture the Castle*. I had to finish the story on my own, mouthing the words, trying in some way to communicate them to her.

The spa day in February was a real treat for both of us and it felt like I had almost got my daughter back. She had to have her syringe driver taken down for the day and rely on intermittent injections. It was a long drive and I had researched the disabled facilities. But she walked in and all day she walked from room to room unaided, enjoying the different sensations of heat and water. She was very sad that she found she couldn't float in the outdoor heated pool but enjoyed the experience of the warm water and cold air. At the end of the day, she even wanted to go and eat in a restaurant, though she hardly ate any of her meal. But she had walked all day and had not vomited and it was a very relaxing experience. Did she enjoy these things and yet have the knowledge that she would never do them again? I don't know how she could bear that.

As she got sicker, my role slipped into more of a carer one. I had to dress her – and often felt her sharp tongue again when I couldn't find the right T-shirt or tights –and help her wash. She always cleaned her teeth at night with one of those timed electric brushes that I can't be bothered to wait for, and continued to do so until about a week before her death. Baths were a treat and we tried all sorts of systems to get her in and out and wash her hair whilst trying to keep two syringe drivers dry. Eventually, one day I couldn't get her out of the bath and after a huge effort and some back damage, I decided that I could no longer bath her. Luckily, the hospice had great baths and she could use them when an inpatient or at the day centre. She took each small defeat in her fight to keep her independence hard but always seemed to bounce back to accept the shrinking of her world.

Thus, our relationship subtly changed. I tried very hard to be primarily a mum as well as a carer. She sometimes got upset that I wasn't just a mum but neither of us wanted to give over the carer role to a stranger so she had to accept it. During the last two weeks of her life, Rose knew that she was close to death. She tried very hard to be around us in the living room but it was too uncomfortable for her so she stayed in bed. I spent more and more time sitting with her or lying next to her. She didn't want to talk much, so we had no 'farewell' conversations. I hope she knew the depth of my love for her and that her family, and some of her friends, would not ever forget her.

CHAPTER 14

After life has ended

The day after her death, a Monday, the funeral directors contacted me. This did not start well: the person who called said, "I believe we have your mother with us." My response was, as you can imagine, rather terse. I know that it was an unusual case and that people aren't always as careful as they should be, but I was very annoyed by this – I was very stressed and every little thing that went wrong seemed to deepen the physical pain of loss I felt. The next day, Harriet and I chose a dress for Rose to wear, one we had particularly liked her in. When I took it to the funeral directors so they could dress her in it, the same person exclaimed, "What, no knickers! Don't you think she should have some knickers?" She looked genuinely shocked. I felt like laughing and giving a snappy retort but controlled myself.

The next hurdle was the Coroner's Office. The Coroner's Officer rang me and took some details. They had to be informed of the death as mesothelioma is an industrial disease. I gave the officer a brief synopsis and he said he would relay that to the Coroner but that there shouldn't be a problem. He rang back about half an hour later and said the Coroner wanted a post-mortem. To give him his due, I don't think he agreed with this decision and I didn't shoot the messenger. But I was upset, which he picked up. I explained that this was a histological diagnosis and, therefore, nothing could be gained from a PM. The officer said that the Coroner was concerned that she was 'so young and we don't know where she contracted it'. I said that a PM would not give an answer to that. As for being 'so young', I explained that, for whatever reason, this particular kind of mesothelioma seemed to occur in young women. I felt a little as if I was being accused of something. I asked the officer to contact the respiratory consultant and also sent over some clinic letters which mentioned the diagnosis from the biopsy. To his credit, he argued my case and the next day the Coroner had changed his mind. Yet again, I felt this was an occasion where if I hadn't been a doctor then a post-mortem would have been done, at great emotional cost to me as a mother. It made me sad, and angry, that another professional was too ignorant, or too lazy, to make a decision before gaining the full picture and asking for the evidence.

After this, things went smoothly. The hospice staff very kindly arranged for all the equipment that had helped Rose be cared for in her flat, to be collected the next day. I asked Rose's close friends if they wanted to come around and choose any of her jewellery or clothes or furniture. They came and I think they felt very awkward, but once they started, they seemed to quite enjoy the process and found it therapeutic. David and Harriet cleared out all the rest of the things in Rose's bedroom and discovered she had been a real hoarder. She had kept rail tickets, cards, and there was even a box full of letters that had come for the previous tenants! They took what they could to the local charity shops. It was really helpful to me that they did this.

There were over 200 people at Rose's funeral at her church in Headington. With the wonders of social media, people from all her previous lives were contacted and many came. Harriet's father designed the 'order of service', using photos of Rose's favourite places and he took it on himself to find some poems relevant to all those places. I was very touched by this. Rose had chosen the songs and readings with George, her great friend, and I arranged for a friend to start the service with Beethoven's Piano Sonata, Pathétique, the second movement, which Rose used to play. To try and lift the mood at the end I chose *My Favourite Things* from *The Sound of Music*, one of Rose's favourite films. My brother read a eulogy I had written and George read one she had written.

We arranged for Rose to be buried in the Woodland Burial Ground just outside Cambridge and Bob's brother, a retired bishop in the USA, and his wife, came and conducted some of the brief ceremony there. Thus, Cambridge, which was always dearer to her heart than Oxford, received her back. Many of our friends from around the country, and outside it, came to one or both of the ceremonies to support us which was lovely. We received over 80 cards of condolence, which was a testament to how many lives Rose had deeply touched.

The next hurdle came in September when the inquest took place. As mesothelioma is a designated industrial disease, there has to be an inquest. I had written a timeline of Rose's life, where she lived, went to school and university and where she had worked. Included in this was a six-month period when she had worked in Argentina, building a school. I made a comment that this may have been the source of the asbestos as there were no other obvious candidates. Bob and I went to the inquest in Oxford. There were two other people in the room. The Coroner went through the usual procedure of reading some extracts from the medical reports and my timeline. He asked me about the time in Argentina and I said that I had absolutely no proof but that I thought it should be noted for epidemiological reasons – someone researching this disease in younger people may come across a similar case. The Coroner agreed to put a note in the narrative, but not in the cause of death. The next thing I know, someone tells me that it is on the BBC website. One of the people had been from the BBC. The other was a journalist and they rang me the next day to ask permission to write an article and include a photograph from the Oxford Neurosciences website. I discussed a bit about the Argentina trip but said why I had mentioned it and that there was no proof. The journalist distributed the story to other papers and the article was in *The Oxford Times* and then the *Daily Mail*. I was angry to see that the *Mail* had used photographs from Rose's Facebook page and that the headline sensationalised the Argentina story. Then I was rung by a reporter from *The Times*. He seemed reasonable and was checking things before he wrote his article. I asked him not to make a big thing about the Argentina trip as I had no proof and I didn't want people to be put off doing gap years. He agreed but said that he didn't write the headlines. Needless to say, the headline was 'Woman killed by asbestos years after gap year project'. The article itself was well written and reported what I had said fairly, but it made me feel that I should never have talked to them in the first place. Then ITV rang wanting to do an interview. I said that I might, but that I would not if they were going to concentrate on the gap year. The reporter said he would check with his editors but never got back to me.

I thought it was important to raise the issue of mesothelioma and I asked that they put the Just Giving link in the reports so that at least some more money might be raised. But the whole episode made me feel that I had no control and made me gloomy.

We finally got Probate over Rose's estate which meant we could sell her flat and arrange for the donations of her compensation money to the three things that I thought she would approve of: her church, the hospice in Oxford, Sobell House, and the research centre for mesothelioma at Imperial College.

David used the money from his sister's pension to buy a house around the corner from us, something he would never have been able to do without that money. I slowly restarted my different streams of work but felt that I could not go back to doing general practice in the usual way, so have chosen a different line of clinical work where I will not encounter and get involved in the various things, big and small, that cause distress to patients. I don't feel I have that strength at the moment, and I don't know if I can trust my ability to be empathetic towards people whose problems are, in the grand scheme of things, trivial.

And what of grief? I have learnt something about this. I witnessed Rose's grief at losing the life she loved bit by bit over nine months. I really did not feel able to console her in this grief but tried to just be there when she wanted me to be. I saw her go through the phases, of denial, of anger and of acceptance. I don't think she really 'allowed' anyone into this grief to help her, but I think she understood the love and support that was coming her way. I cannot speak of my family's grief because we do not talk about Rose in that way. In terms of myself, I have found that I can function, can work, can laugh and be a support to others. But underneath all this, I have felt as if I am walking on the edge of a cliff and that the smallest thing will push me over; like I am a balloon that is overinflated and ready to burst. Others can help or can make the pressure greater depending on what they say. Anyone who says "I know how you feel" will get a cool reception, unless they have gone through the experience of losing a child. Many say, "I cannot imagine what you are going through" or "I have been thinking about you a lot", and this is helpful, but often makes me cry. There are those who say nothing, and I think, do they know? How can you know and say nothing? And there was one who wrote a line of condolence on their Christmas card followed by a full page of what their children were , complete with happy family photograph. I'm afraid they did not get a card from me.

When Rose was alive everything was about her, not about me. Now I think it should be about me and my family. I am grateful to all the true friends who came to Oxford, listened to me and did what they could to help, practically and emotionally. As someone who always had to be in control of their emotions and not talk readily about themselves, I decided to see a therapist where I could talk and cry without burdening my friends. That has been useful and the balloon is more stable. We will soon be moving out of the year that Rose died, and I am not sure how that will be. People's expectations of how my grief manifests itself may change. People may stop talking about her so much. She may slip out of my mind one day, as not a day has gone by when I don't think of her so far. That is a frightening thought. I am frightened that I may forget her. Of course, that will never happen, not when your own child dies. There will always be events that will make us think of Rose. Apart from birthdays and death days, there will be the birth of her nieces and nephews, events in the life of friends and family when we will imagine her being there to share them. We will always miss her.

CHAPTER 15
The future of medicine

Although this book has been a personal journey for me, I have also tried to widen out the issues I faced to inform the debates in the world of medicine at this point in time. The communication skills of doctors have always been of interest to me and I am heartened to have witnessed some very skilful doctors on this journey. Younger doctors now have to spend a part of their training developing these skills, a path that was emblazoned by general practice. I also encountered some clinicians who seemed completely unaware of the effect their poor skills had on their patient. I think the issue of communication skills is quite separate from that of empathy: an empathic doctor can communicate poorly and a good communicator is not necessarily empathic.

Personally, I have always equated general practice with acting, just as I did in my previous career of teaching. Whatever a patient is telling us, we need to put on an act in order to respond appropriately. I can often recall listening to a patient's most intimate details, thinking, 'I really don't want to hear this', but having to respond to them in what I believed to be an appropriate way. The exam that doctors need to pass to become GPs and members of the Royal College of General Practitioners includes a 'surgery' where actors play the part of patients (and they are very good!) and challenge the trainees with some complicated and sometimes ethically difficult scenarios. Preparing trainees for this and watching their real consultations (often by video) is an extraordinarily useful tool in developing communication skills. Hospital doctors do not have such a rigorous training and testing, but communication skills are now included in their assessments.

As I have intimated throughout the book, some of my previously held beliefs about good communication and empathy have been challenged by this experience of Rose's illness. I am no longer in a situation where I can discuss and develop these ideas – I am no longer a trainer of GPs and am no longer part of a Practice. I hope that doctors reading this will reflect on the ways they communicate and will explore the meaning of empathy. Hopefully, they will take some new ideas into their practice as a result of this story of Rose's journey.

Central to this story is also the fact that a diagnosis of mesothelioma is a death sentence. In this day and age, for a cancer to be completely incurable is very rare. I had an interesting discussion with Professor Cookson at the Mesothelioma Research Unit at Imperial College where I donated some of Rose's compensation money. He said that, in his opinion, the research into mesothelioma has been delayed by the fact that it was mainly a 'working class' cancer, that is, it mainly affected workers who were involved in mining asbestos or using it in the building trade. That rang true to me and I remembered the media interest in Rose's case: a young professional woman getting such a disease is much more newsworthy. At least her case may have raised the profile of this disease. Professor Cookson's research has mainly concerned asthma but he is also exploring the genomic sequencing of lung cancers, including mesothelioma. This means that the cells from the tumour are taken and the DNA sequenced. This may lead to treatments that specifically target those genes. It may be possible, through his connections with other institutions, to have Rose's mesothelioma cells sequenced. This may be a small contribution to finding treatments for mesothelioma.

To return to Rose's story, I have included a short chapter on Assisted Dying. I cannot remember ever discussing this issue with Rose before her illness, but we may well have done as she was very interested in discussing topics of the day. Towards the end of her life, I was struck by her obvious wish, however mildly proposed, for her life to end. It surprised me because of her strong faith, but I may be projecting onto her the memories of my upbringing as a Catholic where the belief was that people must bear suffering as God has a reason for it. There is no doubt in my mind that if assisted dying had been legal in this country, she would have seriously contemplated it. I don't believe that my opinion on this matter has any more value than anyone else's, but I do believe that if others had experienced anything like the physical and psychological distress of the terminal illness of a loved one, then the law might be changed. The debate needs to continue.

Rose was so lucky to have district nurses who came every day and a GP who was her designated doctor. She also had palliative care nurses and occupational therapists who all came around to offer their expertise and practical help. When I was a GP partner, five years ago, we had meetings every week with district nurses, health visitors, and occasionally physiotherapists, occupational therapists, psychiatrists and social workers. In these meetings we would discuss our palliative care patients, vulnerable patients and children in need. My work now as a Specialist Advisor on Care Quality Commission (CQC), doing inspections of general practice, reveals a disintegration of the Primary Care System. GPs no longer know their patients as well as they did because they have to design a system for dealing with patient demand and government targets. This works against continuity of care. District nurses no longer attend meetings, nor do health visitors and the rest of the team unless the Practice makes a huge effort to maintain these links in the face of shortages of staff and reorganisation of underfunded services. The most valuable part of general practice is threatened, and I believe that unless something is done to turn things around, I will not receive the kind of care Rose received when it is my time to be cared for at the end of my life.

Since writing this book the COVID-19 pandemic has hit us. General Practice has been forced to make changes, and I doubt it will ever be the General Practice I knew when 'normal' life returns.

Any criticisms I have made are meant to be constructive and educational. The pandemic has revealed our clinicians to be dedicated, caring and brave.

EPILOGUE

I have started to see patients again, in a slightly different role, and I am enjoying it. I thought that I would never be able to do so, that I could not cope with listening to people's trivial problems (not trivial to them, I know, but trivial in the grand scheme of things). But I find that I have retained some of my 'empathy', whatever that now means, and am still a good actor, a good listener, and a good doctor.

I don't know how this grief will behave, when I can go a day without a sudden deep pain when I realise that Rose is no longer alive, instead of just in another city living her life. I am so sad that she had no children – selfish of me, I know – but hope that I will see bits of her in my son's children.

I hope I will maintain contact with her close friends, although that will bring its own sadness. But one day we will be able to talk and laugh about her, remembering her many wonderful attributes and her propensity for stubbornness and perversity. I believe that it is important for doctors and clinicians to have an insight into the extraordinary power they have to influence how people cope with illness and despair. I also would like to donate more money to the research, and to the hospice. I am not a writer; I am a doctor and a mother with a story to tell and I hope that this story will touch the readers in many different ways.

Printed in Great Britain
by Amazon